QUEST FOR THE KASBAH

"Rarely in this day and age do we find a true Renaissance man—someone who engages with equal success in all spheres: physical, political, and literary. Richard Bangs is just such a man."

FRANCIS FIGART, Editor, *Modern Traveler* Magazine

RICHARD BANGS

ALSO BY RICHARD BANGS

QUEST FOR THE KASBAH

DISCOVER THE HEART OF MOROCCO WITH THE WORLD'S FOREMOST EXPLORER!

RICHARD BANGS

Open Road Publishing

Open Road Publishing

P.O. Box 284, Cold Spring Harbor, NY 11724
www.openroadguides.com

Front cover photo courtesy of Lucie Debelkova
(www.luciedebelkova.com).
Back cover photo courtesy of Small World Productions.

To the three walls of my citadel—Walker, Laura and Jasper

CONTENTS

ACKNOWLEDGMENTS

It takes a ksar to craft an enterprise such as this, and there are so many in the village of Morocco to thank for helping hands, warm hearts and hot mint tea.

Shukran first to Abdelhamid Addou, the CEO of the Moroccan National Tourist Office, who helped make this original concept into a reality. And alongside is Rachid Maaninou, the New York-based director of the same good offices; Zoubida Maataoui, also based in New York; and Chakib El Mokhtar Ghadouani from the Press Departmernt, and Mohammed Moumna from Trade Marketing.

Andre Azoulay, the wise advisor to kings.

Kathy Kriger and Rick's Café in Casablanca; Mehdi El Abbadi and La Maison Bleue in Fès; Restaurant Dar Moha in Marrakech; La Fibule in Casablanca; L'Oasis D'Or at Ait Ben Haddou; Omar Lebbar Gerant; Palais M'Nebhi in Fès; L'Alcazar Bar in the Riad Fès (and the wonderfully accommodating Cezarina Jaussoin); Dar El Ghalia in Fès; Hotel Yasmina in the Todra Gorge; Palais Didi in Meknes; Villa Mandarine in Rabat; Restaurant Le Pin in Midelt, Dar Marjana in Marrakech.

The amazing Randy Weston and his African Rhythms;

Guides Hamza Bouzouzou, Jawad Bizza, Youssef Afallah, Bouziani Mohammed, Rachid Mousklou, Issmail Hossni, Mohammed Mohoub, and Fatima-Zohra El Haqaoui.

Seddik and Mohamed at the Terrasse de Tannerie in Fès; Nicole Debono and the Atelier de Soeurs Franciscaines at the Kasbah Myriem in Midelt; the Cooperative Feminine D'Huile D'Argane;

Drivers Ahmed El Abdi, Houcine Bouktib. Mohammed Idles, and Boukhriss A. Majid, and cameleer Ahmed Fayou.

The Hotel Royal Mansour, Casablanca; The Golden Tulip Farah, Casablanca; Harmonia Hotels & Resorts; Jnan Palace Hotel in Fès; Hotel Palais Al Ismailia; Cooperative Ajddigue Tidzi, Modern Travel Agency of Rabat; Sentissi Ahmed and the Palais Mnebhi; Imane Zkhiri and the La Sultana Hotel and Spa; Le Berbère Palace Hôtel in Ouarzazate; The Hilton in Rabat; Hotel Ksar Kaissar; Kanz Erremal.

From Spring, O'Brien I want to thank Chris Spring, David Kleinman, Judy Lee, Nora Brossard and Jessica DeConti.

And, I want to thank inspirations and friends Paul Maritz, Jack Croxton, Patty Stonesifer, Mary Buffett, Nick Reynolds and Peter Guber. Also, Lourdes Uribe, who helped in so many ways in the field. Yuval Ron, for his love and performance of Moroccan music. And Suzanne Arbanas, who did a yeowoman's copyedit from Sarajevo.

I want to give special thanks to Mountain Travel Sobek for its continued vision and keenness for all Moroccan adventures, and especially Kristy Larson, Kota Tabuchi, Anne Wood, Nadia LeBon, Kevin Callaghan, and Kim Beck.

And there can be no adventure taken without ExOfficio, the brand of exceptional clothing and gear I have been wearing and punishing to no ill effects for more than twenty years now. I want to especially thank Steve Bendzak, Brady Miller, Karen Sain and Chris Keyes, who have been so key to keeping me in "Clothing for the Adventurous Spirit," and Nancy Fendler from Fendler Communications.

And that goes for my luggage of choice, Eagle Creek, and my tireless footwear from Teva, and my hardy mountain outerwear from Mountain Hardwear and Chris Strasser, and the ever-insightful sunglasses from Brad Abbott at Costa Del Mar.

And a seering thanks to visionary and seer Jonathan Stein, who has travel in his bones, and brought this adventure to the pages you hold in your hands.

A big-screen-sized thanks needs to go to the incredible film crew that captured this odyssey for public television and beyond. It includes executive producer Small World Productions' John Givens; director-writer Patty Conroy; cinematographer extraordinaire Eric Jensen; grip and production coordinator Sara Givens; genius editor-composer-graphics guy and super hyphenate talent David Ris; American Public Television executives Nelsa Gidney and Chris Funkhouser for believing in, distributing, and promoting *Adventures with Purpose* documentaries to the stations; and of course my compass, producer-writer-director, mastermind, moral supporter, and muse, Laura Hubber.

FOREWORD

by Peter Greenberg
NBC Today Show Travel Editor

Every time I think I've traveled the world I'm reminded of how much more I need to experience, and who reminds me of this every time I see him or talk to him? Richard Bangs. From the moment I first met him 25 years ago, I was awed not just by the stamps in his passport, but by his energy and enthusiasm in finding and experiencing not just the special places in the world, but the special moments....moments that need to be shared.

If you believe, like I do, that travel is an experience meant to be shared, and great travel is an experience meant to be shared with someone you love, then Richard has a special place in history, because he shares those experiences. I vividly remember sitting and talking with him back in 1984, and my sense of awe and amazement as he described for me in intimate detail how he went down the Omo River in Ethiopia. He didn't tell the story in a way to impress me (although I was duly impressed). He told me his experiences in a way to *enlist* me in his quest to see not just different places in the world, but the world in an entirely different way.

His was — and is — the search for subtlety, for nuance, for small but pivotal moments that exist on the threshold of history, and a continuing dream of discovery and renewal.

With Richard, the dream becomes reality.

And the latest reality is Morocco, which finds itself at the intersection of history and the extremes of perception and reality. It is a potent description of a place that has defied history while making it.

Sadly, too many of us have not been there. And too many more of us simply visualize Morocco as a bizarre combination of the movie *Casablanca* and a seductive caricature of a Hope/Crosby "road" movie.

Richard is quick and effective in disabusing us of those stereotypical notions.

Any time a book can tear down stereotypes and encourage you to do so at the same time, that is a book worth reading. So much of what is called travel writing is nothing more than glossy beauty shots of a place that cannot ever convey the true essence of a destination, let alone its hidden character, textures, style and perhaps most important, what it means to you: what it gives you and what you take away from your journey.

Of course there is always the hope of romance associated with great travel. That, coupled with adventure is — at least to me — at the very core of the motivation to travel. But the love affair here is with unreported history and an explanation of it all.

Richard taught me a long time ago that it's not enough to simply visit a place and observe its iconic features from a distance. That's just checking something off some master — and in the end irrelevant — list. You need to touch your destination, feel it, inhale it in proper cultural and historical persepctive. Travel, after all is a process—and if you can understand the process and the history that came before you, then you can appreciate the experience.

And then you need to tell people abouit it.

That's the beauty of how Richard Bangs approaches all of his voyages.

And now, it's a trip to and through the Kasbah.

Throughout history, Morocco was really all about travel, and travelers. It was astop on the way to somewhere else, a hub and spoke from which to seek riches and adventure elsewhere. And today it has become a rich adventure destination in and of itself.

The history Richard tells us is one of almost accidental evolution—how Morocco has become a surprising paragon of tolerance and now embraces different cultures, religions and ideas. And it's all because of the Kasbah, which started as a fortified way station for the caravans heading to the north or east, or south through the Western Sahara. For brief, calming moments, the Kasbah allowed its visitors to feel safe and secure, and in the process to open their minds to the diversity of travelers and traders, to their gods and deities, their fears and hopes.

And somehow, the modern Kasbah embraces the same values. It is an improbable but remarkable journey, and once again Richard Bangs invites us along. There are life lessons to be learned here, perhaps even applied. But again, and most important, Richard doesn't just impress me...He *enlists* me on his latest quest. As always, I'm so glad I'm on this trip.

INTRODUCTION

Dateline: Cradle of Man, Africa

On the 18th day of the expedition—an attempt at the first descent of the Omo River in Ethiopia—we sighted tidy fields of corn and sorghum on the west bank, nodding in a breeze, and a large needlelike dugout canoe hollowed from a tree moored at the bank. Then we spied half a dozen hemispherical huts, dotted aimlessly like molehills on the bank...our first village. Several women who were winnowing grain stopped mid-toss, dropped their huge wicker trays, grabbed their children and ran into to their windowless beehives. The men cautiously stepped down to greet us. Regal in simple robes of beaten bark and ivory bracelets, they stood quietly, leaning on the butt-end of seven-foot spears, waiting. They were Nilotic, with tall, lithe bodies and features much finer than the Bantu tribes to the south. It was these peoples, some ethno-anthropologists believe, who thousands of years ago wandered across the continent and become the first Berbers of what is today the Kingdom of Morocco.

Each man had plucked out all the hairs on his head, save little weaved tufts on the frontal lobe, braided and tied with colored beads and pointing upwards like antennae. All of them had their share of decorative scar tissue (*keloids*) on their shoulders, stomachs, arms and faces. All were uncircumcised, and we envied them the size of their genitalia. A few had smeared their skins with ashes, a natural sunscreen. It was, perhaps, a first contact, as these people lived in the geographical and cultural formaldehyde of seclusion for centuries, and had no connection with a country called Ethiopia; as we later learned from anthropologist David Turton, there were no previous recorded encounters with outsiders. We smiled, made friendly hand gestures, and offered gifts of salt, soap, sugar, cigarettes and fishhooks, and they warily accepted all. When I offered an Ethiopian coin with Haile Selassie's visage stamped on the front, the leader looked at for a long time, rubbed his thumb over the face, turned it over, and then gave it back to me...he had no idea what money was, and could think of no use.

This was, indeed, a primitive place. The year before, a hundred and fifty miles downstream, near the Kenyan border, paleontologists discovered a group of hominid fossils about three million years old, almost double the earliest dated fossils to that point. It was easy to imagine here: the Garden of Eden, the Cradle of Man, the Font of Life...

Our crude maps showed only two ways to exit the Omo River: floating all the way into Kenya, to the soda waters of Africa's second largest lake, where the river flows in and nothing flows out; or, by hiking 25 miles up a tributary called the Mui River until reaching an airstrip that served a C-47 that brought supplies in once a week to a swath of wilderness that is a game park in development. The former option would require an extra two weeks, as the Omo goosenecked for 200 torpid miles, with upstream winds, before effluing into Lake Turkana, and we were down to our last couple days of food. Even if we could make it to Turkana, there was nothing there, save the biggest single population of Nile crocs in the world, some 14,000 by recent estimates. Eight years earlier a palm-log "hotel" was built 100 miles down the lake from the Ethiopian border. But bandits attacked it one night, killing the manager and a Catholic priest who was the sole guest. They captured a third man, an Italian driver named Tony, and forced him to drive the hotel Land Rover until it ran out of gas. Rumor had it that after killing Tony they skinned him, and members of the gang were reputed to be wearing pieces of his skin to this day. The hotel never reopened.

So, we had to find the Mui River. The canyon had opened to a valley, and the river had taken a sharp turn to the south past the Maji Mountains, and was littered with islands. Matching compass bearings with our map we knew we were in the general area, across from a region cryptically marked as the "Plain of Death." At every tributary on the eastern bank we would stop and hike up a ways to see if it might fit the tracings on the topos. But every tributary turned the wrong way, or didn't seem to carry enough water to qualify as the Mui "River." Some came close, and we debated if we should commit to an extended survey, which would cost days when we were down to hours of food supply. But, we always voted to continue. If we missed the Mui, we figured we could starve to death. The stakes were suddenly high.

On day 23 my friend Lew Greenwald was rowing. There were just four of us left on the expedition. We had started with seven, but three abandoned the journey several days upstream, at the last bridge crossing, believing the expedition would become lost entering *aqua incognito* downstream. I was crouched in the bow, lethargic from the heat, calluses burning, given up swatting tsetse flies. I glanced over to the eastern bank and saw beneath the shiny dark leaves of a spreading fig tree a clear creek spilling into the Omo, but we were past it. "Lew...pull in!" I yelled. He turned the raft, and bent his back to fight the current and get the boat to shore. George and Diane were upstream, saw our maneuver, and followed suit. Lew pulled in several yards down from the confluence. A missed glance, another few minutes, and we would have passed it.

This must be it, we all agreed, though none was certain. We agreed that George Fuller, our expedition doctor, and his wife, Diane would camp at the confluence and wait with the gear, while Lew and I would hike up the tributary and hopefully find the Mui River Camp and airstrip. We had two cans of tuna left, and split them between our two parties, and Lew and I set out. For hours we splashed up the clear river, finding no sign of any human presence. Straw-flecked elephant dung, electric with flies, littered the banks. At one point we turned at a bend in the river and found ourselves face-to-face with a Nilotic buffalo, a mean-spirited beast, heavy of hoof and horn, which usually charges first and never asks questions. He glowered with almost tangible menace, pawed the ground and snorted short Hemingway sentences, resonant with ill will. We beat a quick retreat to the woods, and wandered among the ficus and tamarinds. We wandered for hours. Still, no sign of a camp or trail or strip. At sunset, we decided to climb trees, and we each shimmied up as far as we could go on separate trunks.

But we could see nothing...just the midnight green of endless primary forest. Though Jewish, Lew had spent time traveling through North Africa, and had become something of a student of the Muslim world, and his observations and insights would show up at seemingly random moments, such as while hovering atop the arboreal canopy. "Green is the color of Islam," Lew commented, as though that might give us hope. But the ultimate in hopelessness is to be lost, and we were.

We set up our tiny $30 Sears A-frame tent in a tight clump of nettles and bamboo, thinking it would prevent buffaloes or other large wildlife from making unwanted visits. We crawled in, and opened the last can of tuna. As we ate it we reflected on the adventures we had shared since being in Ethiopia, and wondered aloud if they might be our last.

Lew had lent me a dog-eared copy of one of his favorite books a few days earlier, *The Sheltering Sky* by Paul Bowles, a New Yorker who moved to Tangier to write. By candlelight I settled in to read. I couldn't sleep, for fear of what wandered outside the flimsy tent fabric, but also because the novel so engrossed me, its pace moving like its restless characters, a New York couple who dive deep into the Sahara losing identities along the way. It is, in some senses, a travelogue, a moving story on the merits and tragedies of getting lost. Kit and Port Moresby (was he named for the capital of Papua New Guinea, a place that has no roads that allow an exit?) are fleeing their own atomized culture, defraying civilization's claim, pitching themselves into a new and alien landscape, just as Lew and I were doing on the opposite side of the continent. In the novel one of the journeyers makes the ultimate sacrifice of exploration…he dies in a fever in an untried place, a Kasbah in the desert. The other, however, finds some sort of satori in becoming utterly unhinged from home… affirmation in negation; a transcendent ecstasy that can only be found by becoming lost. I loved that notion, and it slid me into dreamless sleep.

I awoke to a rustling, pulled back the tent flap. There, not ten feet away, was a white-buttocksed waterbuck, noshing on breakfast leaves. The delicate animal turned and stared at me, twitching its pointed ears, but continued chewing, showing no signs of fear. "Look, look, look!" I nudged Lew awake. The waterbuck saw Lew's face emerge, and he softly strode towards the tent. Somehow motion seemed frozen as he strolled towards us, pausing a few feet from our portal. Lew gently pulled back the mosquito netting, and extended his hand. Instead of running away, as I expected, the waterbuck walked closer. Lew and the antelope exchanged looks, and touched one another for a second, the black nose nuzzling Lew's big hand. Then the waterbuck quietly stepped back into a stand with leafy branches that hung like waterfalls, and disappeared.

For a few magical moments I didn't harbor any regrets for being lost, didn't begrudge our predicament. I only thought about the unpredictability of nature, and how accepting that can open the mind to surprise and wonder and the delight of serendipity in body Africana.

My stomach growled, and the moment broke. We needed to get going if we were to emerge alive from the Omo Valley. We decided to hike inland from the tributary, as we might be able to see farther from the savanna than from within the dense riparian vegetation. But, as I made my first steps arrows of pain shot up my legs. In high school I had been on the track team, and occasionally would suffer from shin splints. Now, perhaps because I had spent so much time in a raft over the previous weeks, my shins were splinting. It was terribly painful to walk, and I could only do so with a slow limp. To make matters worse, we had to hike through a fence of sharp spicules that lacerated our legs. Lew offered to help me along, and carry my pack, the tent and my canteen. Still, it was tough going.

All day I limped across the savanna, one hand on Lew's shoulder, hunger and exhaustion welling. At one point I stepped on something, and it slithered out into the open. It was a giant rock python, we guessed about 17 feet long. But I was in too much pain and too exhausted to react. It vanished in the undergrowth, and we continued. Late in the day Lew insisted we climb a small hill to see if we might see something. He practically dragged me to the top, and once there I scanned the horizon to all points, and saw herds of Burchell's zebra, bouncing gazelle, a couple of eland and hartebeest, even a running ostrich...but no airstrip...just endless wilderness and wildlife. I was ready to lie down and admit defeat, and I told Lew so. "No, we're gonna be rich and famous...hang in there," he soothed as he continued to look. Then he stopped and grabbed me. "Look...out there." I strained, but saw nothing. "Look, beyond those trees."

And then I saw it...a tiny metallic glint. The sun had lowered enough to send back a flash of reflecting light. It was something man-made. A renewed energy charged through me.

We practically ran down the hill, and made in the direction of the glint. An hour later we summited a small rise, and there in front of us was a thing of phantasmal beauty...a small mud shed that seemed to have grown from the earth, festooned with an aluminum roof. Next to it was a hand-painted sign: "Mui International Airport," and beyond, a rough airstrip cleared from the elephant grass. In the shade of the hut was a sleeping teenage boy, and when we woke him up, he stared as though in the midst of his worst nightmare. He gathered his senses and led us down a path to a small-tented camp beside the Mui River. There we met the park ranger, Mesfin, an Amhara with a Land Rover, and he pulled us into his canvas tent and fed us mountains of millet. Our faces creased as we remembered how good it felt to scratch the elemental itch of hunger. Then, because my leg was still on fire, Mesfin tucked me into my sleeping bag and drove back with Lew to fetch George and Diane Fuller, who had given us up for lost and were preparing to re-launch to cast their fates to the river. For three days we lounged in relative luxury. Mesfin had an old copy of *Reader's Digest*, featuring a piece on 101 ways to make hamburgers, and Lew and I drooled over the pictures, vowing to make every recipe with our return to the U.S. And I reread *The Sheltering Sky*, which now evoked in me an agreeable kind of horror. I turned to Lew and said, "Let's head to Morocco next."

"Yeah…let's get lost there," he widely smiled.

Two days late, the Ethiopian Airlines C-47 flew in, and we made the noisy three-hour flight back to Addis, back up over the magic medley of ravines and valleys that made up the Omo catchment. At a buna bet in the capital, as we alternatively celebrated and repined our return to civilization, we met Ato Hassan, an Ethiopian tour guide, who told us one of his distant relatives was the mother to a great 14th sultan in Morocco. "He's buried in the Chellah gardens near Rabat," he told us. And we began to plot our next adventure.

But we never made it to Morocco. Not long afterwards Lew found himself lost in a whirlpool on the Blue Nile. His raft had wrapped against a basalt wall, and he was washed downstream. He was found the next day, drowned, and was buried beneath a pile of rocks in the river canyon.

1. THE WORLD IS WHAT IT IS

"Kindness can pluck the whiskers of a lion"
—Moroccan proverb, anonymous

We sat on pillows and dipped flat bread into soup. The music of the oud went on, a patterned background for our aimless talk amidst a press of people of many hues and stripes. All the noises of the world were in that room, yet between it all we watched the plucked notes from the pear-shaped instrument curl and fold in the thick air like the smoke of a wood fire.

My son Walker and I were in the restaurant of the Le Tichka Salam Marrakech Hotel, in the shadow of the Atlas Mountains in Morocco, the mountains named for the Greek god condemned to hold up the sky forever. Worn from travel we lingered over the last sips of our respective drinks, he a sugary tea, and me a glass of Toulal Guerrouane, a bright Moroccan red wine. Several yellow and brown cats were sprawled around the room, in positions that mirrored our mood. With muted interest we both looked up as the waiter poured him another cup of sugared mint tea, deftly cascading the brew from three feet above the table.

"Let's head south to the Sahara," I suggested, looking into Walker's young eyes, which caught the light with the prospect.

It seemed an enticing notion, as close as it was. But there was a hitch: the great fence of the Atlas Mountains, which separates the upper body of Africa from the Sahara. We could magic carpet over one of the several passes in a car, but that wouldn't be sporting. After some discussion we decided to trek over the great range, north to south, to the orange sands of the Sahara.

The next day, at the offices of Atlas Sahara Treks, owner Bernard Fabry unrolled a map on his desk, then traced a route with his finger through the Central High Atlas. If we took a four-wheel drive vehicle we could crawl up the Aroundane Mountain and drop down the other side into the Bouguemez Valley, the end of the road. From there we could trek for four days over the Mgoun Pass to the other side. We would reach the road, where we could hire a vehicle to take us to Ouarzazate, the hem of civilization, the gateway to the Sahara.

Bernard would set us up with a guide from the Bouguemez Valley. "But I must warn you," Bernard said in his heavy latte accent, "the weather this time of year is quite unpredictable. Once in the mountains, if a storm comes in, you could be stranded for days, even weeks."

Groggy and feeling guilty for being a few minutes late in a culture that values the elasticity of time, we stumbled into the lobby of the Hotel El Andalous at 6:10 A.M. An hour later our guide arrived along with a new Land Rover Defender. He was twenty-two-year-old Rachid Mousklou, who studied geology for two years at the University of Marrakech, and recently, when not guiding, had been teaching other guides about the rocks and birds in the region. He was in some demand, as he spoke five languages: English, German, French, Arabic and Berber. He had the glassy black eyes of a doll, with little expression (accented by his hat) and an arched forehead. Five hours later we were wending our way up the juniper-line mountain, surging into the snow line. We lunched at the Tizi n' Tirghist Pass (2,629'), then began the long descent into the Bouguemez Valley. The landscape was denuded, most of the trees felled long ago by Berber women collecting firewood. Occasionally, though, we passed a replanting grove filled with slender black cypress, often topped by magpies that shared the same dull color of the mountain's south side.

Our first Berber encounter was in the village of Iframe, where Mohammed, a friend of Rachid's, bounded out to greet us in his new Nikes, a pair of Levis, a fleece jacket, and the same arched face. He invited us inside for some sweet tea and flinty exchanges with Rachid we couldn't comprehend.

An hour later we continued the journey to the sole hotel in the valley, the Dar Itarane (House of Stars), in the mud-walled village of Imelghas. It was a lovely and lonely place, and because it was December, we were the only guests. We staked out a spot in the large dining room, beneath a cedar ceiling encircled by verses from the Koran, and in front of the fireplace. This was our base camp.

As the light leached from the sky, over oily vegetable soup and lumps of half-cooked lamb fat, Rachid told us he had been speaking to the villagers. He said they recommended we not attempt the Mgoun Pass. It was too dangerous that time of year, the weather too unpredictable. He suggested we hike in the other direction, to his father's valley, as an alternative. I unrolled the map, traced the intended route for Rachid, and told him I thought we should give it a go. After all, I had for many years been a professional guide, and if the conditions were deemed too dangerous, we would simply turn around. I knew and usually practiced that rule. I was certain we could make it.

Rachid looked at us. "Inscha'allah," he replied with a shrug, and left the room for the night.

Sharp morning light filled the room, the polished floor tiles reflecting the sun onto the ceiling as if they were water. We adjourned to an adjacent room for a breakfast of lemongrass tea and round bread. The way some Westerners watch television while they eat...looking up to the TV and down to take a bite and back up, that was how Rachid watched the valley out the window while he ate his breakfast. He seemed hooked on the plot and didn't want to miss a thing.

After the light repast we decided to explore the valley and stretch our legs before attempting the first pass.

We wandered among the fields of potatoes, apples, corn and wheat, through several of the twenty-five villages in the valley. Rachid was our cicerone, but for someone so knowledgeable, he was surprisingly reticent. He stated the obvious, that the valley was once under the sea. "Sedimentary, my dear Rachid." He then led us toward a dramatic swirl of earth that strategically over-looked the valley. We scratched our way up the steep mesa and into a two-hundred-year-old shrine, Sidi Moussa. It was an intriguing piece of architecture, cube-modular with several tortu-ous passageways. It had served multiple purposes over the ages, Rachid told me when I asked directly. It was a sort of Kasbah, in that it served as a watchtower and fort, but also a winter storage depot, a grave site for the high and holy, and most important, the home of a mountain god, a spirit who not only protected but helped fertilize women.

According to legend, a woman who was having problems becoming pregnant had to visit Sidi Moussa on three Thursday nights in a row and spend the night. On the fourth night she had to bring a black sheep or other animal to sacrifice, and would then find herself pregnant. Back in Marrakech, Bernard Fabry had told me of this myth, and said he thought there was a simpler explanation. He asked me to notice how similar everyone in the valley looked, and then to note the arched face of the caretaker at Sidi Moussa.

As we walked around the periphery of this belvedere, Rachid looked across the valley to Jbel Waogoulzat, the mountain we were scheduled to climb the next day. It looked like a knee drawn up under a huge sheet. With a staccato gesture he pointed to a faint zigzag in the snow, and uttered that that was our trail. Then he grimaced.

We continued our hike to the valley's main village, Tabant, where a bar stood next to a former French administrative building. Outside a man sat on a white plastic chair, reading a paper, sipping a cup of tea. It looked very much like a scene outside any Paris café, only here the man's face was hidden deep in the recesses of his pointed *burnoose*, looking like Alec Guinness in *Star Wars*. We wandered in, and in front of a blaring TV, a boy, younger than Walker, was watching a racy dance number on an Indian version of MTV. Over in the corner a group of teens was playing Foosball on a table on which the playing field was plastered with the famous nude shot of Marilyn Monroe that appeared in the first issue of *Playboy.*

That evening Rachid told us a superstition in the valley held that people sometimes turn into animals, and that his grandfather, who lived to be 110, was transformed into a mule. Then Rachid again tried to talk us out of attempting our journey, citing the weather. The weather had been fine to this point, I replied, sunny and cloudless. What was the problem? Rachid sulked. I wondered if the animal transformation thing could be hereditary.

At daybreak we were up and packed, and in the compound was an eagle-faced man named Ahmed and his mule with no name. After he strapped on our baggage, as well as food, cooking materials, and sleeping blankets, there was then a steady chugging torrent of urine—the mule's—pounding the baked earth. It was time to head out. Rachid was silent as we made our way up a trail named "The Ambusher." This was one of the caravan passages that enabled the transport of dates, henna, gold and salt between the Sahara and ports in the north. Slowly, we wound up the pass through several biblical-looking villages, where men with wrapped heads and flowing robes milled about in an ancient way, up through groves of juniper and into the snow, following in the footsteps of our nameless mule. The winter light was diffused and slanted, existing in its own illumination, fire filtered through water. Edith Wharton described it as a light of "preternatural purity which gives a foretaste of mirage…that light in which magic becomes real, and which helps to understand how, to people living in such atmosphere, the boundary between fact and dream perpetually fluctuates."

At one point the mule slipped in the snow and almost fell. If the mule broke a leg, he would have to be shot, and Ahmed would lose his greatest asset. This would not do, so Ahmet unloaded the two largest bags and set them in the snow. I wondered what his plan was as he continued up the hill, leaving behind two of my bags. It wasn't until we were close to the crest that I realized my money, passport, and air tickets were in one of the bags left in the snow. I felt a stab of panic, but I was too exhausted to backtrack.

After six hours of continuous walking we crested the Tizi-n-Ait Imi Pass, also known as "The Pass of the Sheep with Black Eyes," and were faced with the stunning white comb of the Mgoun, across the next valley. The wind was howling, and as I pulled on my wool hat, Rachid wrapped his head in his blue *chechia,* a Berber head scarf. We all stooped behind a large rock and unpacked our lunch: cheese, yellow apples, oily black olives, walnuts, hard-boiled eggs and bread. While noshing, Rachid and Ahmed scrambled back down the mountain, returning some minutes later with my missing bags on their shoulders. Then Rachid pointed to some filmy clouds smearing the distance and somberly said, "I think we must go back. The clouds mean bad weather." But as I surveyed the sky I saw that clouds were in the north, while the wind was blowing from the south, the direction we were headed. In fact, the sky ahead was a brilliant blue, so clear a passing jet left contrails like the score of a diamond on a pane of glass. "Rachid," I protested, "the clouds are behind us, and moving away. The weather looks fine in front. I say we should just keep going. How far to the village where we will spend the night?"

"Four hours. But we shouldn't go on. It is too dangerous."

What was his hidden agenda? "I insist. We can do it. There is no reason to turn back," I said, resolutely shouldering my pack and starting down the trail, Walker a few steps behind. With more reluctance than the mule, Rachid followed.

It was an easy descent into the Mgoun Valley, and soon we were walking alongside the crisp Mgoun River. In every direction the view was extravagant, like how I imagined James Hilton's Shangri-la. At one point we passed a series of caves across the river, with crude wooden ladders leading into the darkness. It looked like an Anasazi granary. An hour later we passed a Kasbah, Tighremt-n-Ahmed, which guarded the confluence of a tributary. Its walls looked like freshly-baked gingerbread, as though we could break off a piece and eat it. But Rachid said its walls were sturdy, and had weathered time and attacks of all kinds, including weather. He said that Morocco had over a thousand such Kasbahs (from the Arabic *qasaba*, or citadel), the most authentic architectural vestiges of Morocco's long and glorious history. And, he said, the Kasbahs, more than anything, helped Morocco evolve into a state of strong identity. I didn't quite understand how he drew a line from a mud fortress to national identity, but I was provoked with the concept and wanted to revisit when we were in a more relaxed setting, as we were now chasing darkness.

Thirty minutes later we stumbled into the Hopi-like village of Talat Righane, where the low ochre-colored houses with mud-packed straw roofs seemed to have sprung from the ground. The people here were of the Aitatta tribe, a nomadic Berber confederation that wandered into this valley ages ago, and stayed. All the men wore dun-colored *burnooses*. The women, with their open, confident faces, were intricately tattooed with indigo designs on their foreheads and henna-stained palms and fingers. Pendulum earrings of silver, turquoise and amber swung as they walked and spoke. As for clothing, they only wore black, blue and red.

Rachid spoke with one of the village elders, and after a while we were led though a heavy wooden horseshoe-shaped door into a small compound, then up the stairs to a narrow room lined with Berber carpets and pillows. This was to be our room, he indicated, and brought in piles of sheep-wool blankets.

After settling in, we stepped outside to admire the landscape. It was the moment of twilight when light objects seem unnaturally bright, and the others restfully dark. Even in my pile sweater and down jacket I still felt the cold, like a piece of metal inside me, yet the villagers, in their cotton clothes, didn't seem to notice. One woman stepped up to Rachid with her small son at her side, and then pulled the child's pant leg up to reveal a festering wound the size of a half-dollar on his calf. "What is it?" I asked Rachid.

"A dog bite." There were a half dozen Atlas sheepherder dogs within sight, a couple barking frenetically at our presence.

"Well, isn't there a doctor she can see?" Walker asked.

"Not in this valley. She would have to climb over the pass to where we came from, but she won't because it would take two days, and she doesn't want to spend the money for medicine. But I have a medical kit, I can help."

But the woman and small boy were already wandering away. Rachid turned on his heel and chased them. The cold wind blew away the last feeble strands of light.

That night Walker and I huddled by a small propane lamp, extracting what little warmth it generated. Ahmed brought us tea and tajine in a trumpet-shaped lid, sliced vegetables and pieces of cartilaginous meat cooked over a wood fire, and we chowed down. Then Rachid came in smiling, and said the boy would be fine…he had taken him to the local Kasbah, where he cleaned the wound, administered some oral Amoxicillin, and bandaged the leg. But Rachid's generous mood was fugacious. As he sat down he assumed a guttural mountain tone, and fixed his dark eyes, like the bright backs of captured beetles, on mine. "We can't go on. The villagers say the pass is closed, and it is impossible to proceed."

"Wait a minute. What about the Mgoun River? On the map there is a route that follows the river through a gorge and avoids the pass altogether. Why can't we try that?"

"That, too, is closed. It is impossible to negotiate this time of year. The water is too high."

"C'mon. This is December. This is the slowest time of year for runoff. We've seen the river; it's low, probably the lowest for the season."

"Well, the river in the gorge is still up to your chest, and the water is too cold now. We can't go on."

"How about we just walk downstream tomorrow and check things out?"

After a long silence Rachid took a draw on his Casa Sports cigarette, then replied, "Okay, but then we must turn back. You must promise me that. We can always visit my father's valley." It was a measure of his touching earnestness that he saw nothing even faintly amusing about his reiterative pursuit.

Secretly I conspired to find someone in this remote valley with whom I could communicate, and get a second opinion. That would be my next day's agenda. Like some literary figures before me, I was being pulled to the unknown south, and didn't really consider the consequences. I was prepared to get lost.

It didn't work as I had hoped. I wandered around without Rachid's company, but my phrase books were of no help as nobody spoke a word of French or Arabic. This was truly an isolated demesne. So much so the French were never able to penetrate this valley. There are no photographs of the King, which are in most every shop and building in the rest of the country. Somehow I found this delightful, even though I could not find a soul who could tell me if this journey could be completed. Finally, I began to hike downstream in the direction of the gorge, with Rachid at my heels. As one point I passed several Berber women festooned with amber necklaces, their plaited hair shining with oil and flecked with saffron. Walker pulled out his camera to take a photo, and Rachid held up his hand and stopped the image. "What's wrong?" I asked.

"They believe you'll be taking their souls."

"Will they accept money?"

"That's a bad habit, to offer money to corrupt a culture," he scolded, and Walker put his camera away.

Sometime in the early afternoon I heard the singing voices of women echoing up the canyon. We were entering the village of

El Mrabitine, where Rachid said the greatest singers in Morocco lived. Soon we passed the women, who were in harvest bent, swinging scythes in the fields. They looked up as we passed, and Walker pulled out his camera. They smiled, teeth like bleached desert bones, and Walker fired off several shots. I pulled out a few dirhams and offered to pay, but the women refused the gesture.

In this Old Testament village there is a single shop. Four men loiter out front, a Berber shop quartet. The store offers the usual items of hard biscuits, sweets and dates, and also a can of Coke, which I promptly buy, and share with Walker. Then the shop owner, who had the apple-like cheeks of a man satisfied with his lot, closed his shutters and led us through a labyrinthine set of corridors up to a tea room, where he tore apart green stalks of mint and stuffed them into a little teapot, a garden in a kettle . When Rachid wandered off for a few minutes I desperately tried to communicate with the shop owner, asking about the Mgoun Pass, about the river route, drawing pictures in my notebook. But he didn't understand. When Rachid returned, I closed my notebook and took a sip of tea.

"Are you certain we can't go forward?" I implored Rachid one last time, my voice rising. The exchange was becoming stylized and repetitive, like a belly dance. I suddenly felt a bit foolish with my oft-repeated question. In my twenties I, too, had been a guide, and one of the few unpleasant aspects of the job was having to deal with obnoxious clients who repeatedly demanded something impossible. For a second I was horrified to realize that, just as children become their parents, I had become one of my clients.

"It's time for us to return," Rachid said after a time. It was getting late, and if we weren't going forward, we had to leave then to make it back to Talat Righana. But before we departed I walked down to the river. The air was heavy with the odor of spearmint that grew along the banks. I dipped my hand in its waters. It was cold, and the volume had increased with several tributaries, so much so it looked like it might be navigated with a kayak or small raft. I found myself wishing I had somehow had the foresight to bring a small boat. Then I could have paddled to the Sahara. I shrugged, like Atlas, and turned to head back.

Along the way Rachid broke his usual silence to tell me that he hoped to one day visit the Andes. "What about Mount Everest?" I asked in return. "No," he replied. "The Andes." Unusual, I thought. Every other mountain guide I had ever met dreamed of visiting the Himalayas above all else. There was something about expectations here; they never seemed too high. Happiness is reality minus expectations, goes the Zen saying, but somehow in practice it seemed to work here.

The following day we staggered back into the House of Stars. The weather had been picture perfect, and I was bitter and suspicious about whether we could have completed our journey. When Walker went to download his photos of the village women, he discovered the images were gone, wiped clean by some bug.

Now the dining room, despite a blazing oak fire, seemed stuffy and melancholy. Over couscous Rachid told us that two Moroccan shepherds died trying to cross the Mgoun Pass just last month. He said they started their trek, traveling without mules, and it was a beautiful day. But a sudden storm came in at noon, and they froze to death.

I didn't know whether to believe Rachid. The weather had been so ideal, and if we had continued we would be just one day from completing our crossing.

The next morning I awoke to the sound of giant trees crashing. But that couldn't be right, because the few trees in the valley were slight willows and poplars. I realized then it was thunder. I pulled back the shutters. The sky was black and a huge storm had moved in. It was pouring rain, and lightning streaked across the sky. Fresh snow covered Jbel Waogoulzat, which I could barely make out across the valley. If we had continued, we would have been smack in the middle of the storm.

Four days later we found ourselves in a 1979 Mercedes 2000D taxi climbing the Tizi n' Tichka Pass on the way to Ouarzazate. The road is a feat of engineering engineered by the Foreign Legion in 1936, though I am not inclined to admire it. The weather was still snotty, the storm releasing its last licks. Our driver/guide was Boukhriss A. Majid, a thin thirty-two-year-old playwright and mountain guide with a salient nose. He was in many ways the opposite of Rachid….blithe, informative, passionate. He unfurled poetry, shared history, and spoke of legends as we wended up through the Atlas the easy way. At the top of the pass two tourist buses swerved on the ice and blocked the way. It looked as though we would have to turn back, our journey thwarted again. While waiting by a roadside stand selling red onyx, green agate and black geodes, an oasis of nugacity in an otherwise worthy landscape, a little Berber girl wrapped in a shawl plastered me with a snowball and giggled. Then she offered me a crystal as though some sort of atonement. I reached in my pocket to give her some change, but she shook her head no, and closed my hand over the stone.

Finally, after a couple hours of digging, pushing, yelling, and shoveling sand under the wheels, the buses were freed, and the pass reopened.

We coiled down into a dull, rose landscape, past caravans of women bent over double as they carried their loads of firewood, their faces seamed with fatigue. We passed mules, backs piled high with lumpy, closed sacks, loping down the mountain. And we passed an ancient Kasbah on a hill, with its rammed earth walls and tiny windows. Boukhriss pointed to the fortress and said, "Over 500 people once lived there. It is the structure that gave Morocco its pride and character."

Under a lowering sky we drove through the stout, crenellated walls of the four-star Riam Salam hotel in Ouarzazate, and took a room that sat on the flat roof. From there we could see the sullen sweep of the desert, the tufted tops of date palms soughing in the breeze, the shimmering waters of a river that would somewhere far away find the sea. I checked the map, and found that the currents of the Mgoun River, which I had touched a few days before, spilled into the Dades, which in turn was a tributary of the Drâa River, which flowed by this hotel. We were reunited. And as a white crescent moon began to swim upwards, the waiter brought us our order on an ornate brass tray, and in the soft air we sipped beer and soda at the edge of the Sahara, the sands that prefaced us, and will outlive us. We were out of time. We had a day scheduled in Fès, and then we had to head home for Walker's school. But that meant there was still a chance to get lost.

2. LOST ON A STRAIGHT PATH

"I do not like this city. It is my past and I do not like my past. I have grown up, I have pruned myself back. Fès has quite simply shriveled up. However, I know that as I go deeper into the city it seizes me and makes me entity, quantum, brick among bricks, lizard, dust—without needing to be aware of it. Is it not the city of the Lords?"
–Driss Charibi, *Le Passe Simple*, 1954

The cosmic soup that is the medina of Fès el-Bali (Old Fès) is the largest living Islamic medieval city in the world, and so tendriled and tortuous that even those living just outside the walls often do not enter for fear of getting lost. There are no maps; no street signs. Hell is better organized. It is physical manifestation of a calligraphic arabesque, endless and circular, a maze within a knot inside a honeycomb within a skein within a web. With Walker just a few steps behind we passed beneath a gate of three symmetrical horseshoe arches and kneaded down a smoky, teeming alley, thick with the tintinnabulations and perfumes of North Africa. Sunlight slashed through awnings, zebra-striping merchants hawking brass trays and jewelry. Amidst the fizz and riot something shiny caught my eye, and I turned down a tight cobblestone corridor; but then a bolt of blue silk carried on a shoulder slid past, and I decided to follow. But I had to flatten against a wall as mule bundled with stalks of mint barged by, and watched helpless as the man turned out of sight. I nearly caught up, and chased him through the press as he turned again and again in a labyrinthine route, until one turn too many and he was gone. I turned around and so was Walker. I tried to trace my steps back, back through the thread-like streets to where I had last seen my son, but I couldn't find my way.

Suddenly I was swept up in a river of people, and poured into a side alley. I was in a section of the souq selling mounds of fly-ridden meats. Then one with vivid sculptures of lemons, and then another with neatly-arranged pyramids of dates, figs, nuts, turmeric, paprika, and herbs and spices beyond my ken. I tried to ask directions from shopowners and shoppers alike, but nobody seemed to understand, though all over-smiled and waved me into their shops. Several men bowed slightly, putting their right hands gently on their hearts, as though my predicament touched them as well. I turned left, then right, then right again, and left, then right, right again, left, another left, and then I stopped and simply stood still. The corridors refused to settle. I realized I was lost, and a dizziness set in. But then something else ran through me like a curved dagger…unexpectedly I felt unfettered, as though there were no past, no loads, no directions or guides, just the woozy exotic moment. I chewed on it like a fig, and felt as edged and alive as I could be.

There are many tales of the virtues of becoming lost, from Moses in the wilderness, to Livingstone in Central Africa, Kit Moresby in the Sahara, Shackelton in Antarctica, Herzog on Annapurna. And in some sense whenever someone signs up for an adventure travel trip today there is for many a quest to leave something behind, to become lost in a new place and time, and emerge somehow different. But while there may be a subconscious urge to let go and be lost, more often than not once in the wilderness, in a foreign culture or unfamiliar landscape, a voice reins the opportunity in, and that last step is not taken.

Always there is healthy risk involved in getting lost: the catalogue is thick with those who suffered the ultimate consequences of getting lost, from George Leigh Mallory on Everest to Amelia Earhart over the Pacific, to Teddy Roosevelt, who when he set out to explore the River of Doubt in Brazil, said, "I had to go. It was my last chance to be a boy." He got lost on the Amazon tributary, where he picked up the malaria that led to his premature death.

The man who most influenced my career in exploration, David Livingstone, the great Scottish missionary/explorer, spent thirty years wandering about lost in Africa seeking "God's Highway" (a water passage into the African interior that would allow colonization, the end of Arab slave trading, and Christian conversion of "heathens").

Livingstone died at the age of 59 in the Bangweulu Swamps of Northern Zambia clinging to the delusion he was tracking the course of the Nile. His heart was cut from his body, placed in a box, and buried under an *mpundu* tree, while his body was carried to the coast, and shipped to England. One of his last journal entries reads: "Dear God, I am oppressed that this may, after all, be the Congo. Who would risk their life for that dreadful river?" In fact, he did, and indeed in his lost stupor he had discovered the source of the Congo. Many years later I found myself lost in the Bangweulu Swamps trying to find Livingstone's tree, but did nothing more than muddy my boots.

In 1977 I led one of the first American tourist groups to the People's Republic of China. While in a museum in Shanghai I felt ill and decided to make my way back to the hotel on my own, but promptly got lost. I couldn't read the road signs, or decipher my map. It was forbidden for Chinese to speak with foreigners then, and every time I approached a Mao-suited pedestrian, he skirted away. Finally, an old man who had been a teacher before the 1949 revolution noticed my distress and approached me. In broken English he offered to help, and after showing him my embossed hotel key, he guided me to the front steps. That single gesture remains the headiest memory of that culturally indulgent visit.

A couple years ago I took the concept to a higher plane, joining a "civilized" bike trip through Burgundy, France. While pedaling with the pack past vineyards that produce the world's finest white wines I saw a patch of sunflowers down a lane, and decided to take a detour. Everything was fine as I wound down a lonely road. And then "SWIisssh" and I shuddered to a stop to discover my back tire gone flat. I was several miles off course, and the only sound was the wind nagging through my spokes.

Then one of those providential things happens when lost. A bright-eyed Burgundian stopped his Citroen, inspected my bike, and produced a rusted metal wedge, which he immediately jammed into the bike rim and pulled off my bad tube. As I watched the operation I heard birdsong over my shoulder, the first on the trip, and looked up to see a sky as blue as the Gauloise packet the stranger carried. I felt the hot sun on my face. A lizard posed at the edge of the road, looking like a watercolor. At last the stranger flashed a smile that reached into his cheekbones, and presented my bike. I pulled a wad of francs from my pack, but the stranger furrowed his forehead, put his hands to his chest, palms faced to me, and shook them no. "Bonne route," he said, then motored away. The little tumult was a brief quickener of sensation, and for the first time on the trip I felt unlocked in a way not found in the comfort zone.

Here in Fès while lost in the bazaar I came across a beautiful backgammon set with pieces carved from onyx. I sat with the owner and shared tea in porcelain cups and talked in languages we each didn't understand about its loveliness and its cost. He wore a bucket-shaped, dark red hat with a black silk tassel, what Moroccans call a *tarboosh*, but which others call a Fez. The name may have come from this city, which once produced the dye, made from crimson berries, to color the hat.

Finally, after sending back and forth folds of dirhams, we agreed, without a common language, on a price for the backgammon set, and he placed the set in a camel bag. As I turned to leave I saw Walker step by, and, with some regret, we were reunited. He had enjoyed his own adventure, and was eager to describe the tapestry of sights, the voluptuous smells and sounds; they were the best he had experienced; and the worst. But it was time to head back to the familiar.

We had some time in Casablanca before our flight back to the US, so we headed to a coffee shop, where I pulled out the backgammon set, and we sat down for a game. Like most coffee shops in Morocco, it was crowded and dense with smoke and talk, yet as we began to move our pieces, several strangers gathered about our table and not only watched our game, but gave commentary, not just on the game, but on all the events of the world, or so it seemed. The game lingered, and so did the social scene, which bristled with nowness, a constant and fecund presence. Too soon the Mercedes taxi arrived, and with talk and game interrupted we headed for California.

3. DRINKING FROM WELLS WE DID NOT DIG

"This life is a hospital where every patient is possessed of a desire to change beds."

Charles Baudelaire, *Les Fleurs du Mal*, 1857

Paul Bowles once wrote that North Africans were at peace with themselves, content with their lives. They were satisfied because they didn't ask questions. They were calm, not driven. The American dream, he added, was the dumbest drug.

Sometimes I would put the Moroccan backgammon set under my arms and head to the local coffee shop to play a game with Walker, but it was different here. We played in solitude; nobody seemed interested in our strategy, our moves, our thoughts. I looked around sometimes and watched as the coffee shop became a gathering place of mystic vacancies....everyone seemed enclosed in an electronic wall, be it laptop, BlackBerry, iPod, Kindle or other device. Even though the barista would call us by first name when an order was ready, there was nothing personal about this place anymore, and no room for chance encounters or random bumps. We were unessential to this world, covered in our own cones of silence. It seemed different in Morocco, but perhaps it was just memory playing tricks in the rambling house of my mind.

Shortly thereafter I found myself in New York sitting next to Rachid Maaninou, the newly appointed director of Moroccan Tourism for North America. I shared with him my thoughts that gatherings in the West were changing, becoming more insular, perhaps stronger with primary relationships, with whom we could be in near-constant touch, but at the sacrifice of the "soft relationships" of strangers. I commented that Morocco had seemed different, especially in the markets, medinas and coffee shops, and wondered if there was a cultural differentiation.

Rachid wove his fingers together on his chest and thought for a moment.

"It has to do with the Kasbahs." Despite what I had seen and heard so far of Kasbahs in Morocco, my strongest association was with the character Kit Moresby in *The Sheltering Sky*, a wayward creature, a spoiled bohemian adventuress, with whom I identified in some way, who could easily be written off were it not for her final decision to return to the Kasbah rather than live a life of leisure in New York. So, I didn't really see Rachid's connection, and advancing feather light asked for clarification.

"Our Kasbahs were unique in that they achieved a kind of correspondence between belief and place, between inner and outer landscapes, between protection of family, and openness to traders and travelers. But don't trust me....go see for yourself."

4. MOHAMMED TO THE MOUNTAINS

"Where all is Eden, or a wilderness.
There the large olive rains its amber store
In marble fonts; there grain and flower and fruit
Gush from the earth until the land runs o'er;
But there too many a poison-tree has root,
And midnight listens to the lion's roar,
And long, long deserts scorch the camel's foot
Or heaving whelm the helpless caravan.
And the soil is, so the heart of man."
–Lord Byron, *Don Juan*, 1819-24

And so it is I arrive once again in Morocco, but this time with a different purpose, an attempt to unriddle this concept of the Kasbah as a place that evolved a different way of dealing with the walls of the world.

I arrive in Casablanca after dark, the moon a sliver of lemon rind. Outside the airport I hook up with a driver, Mohammed Idles, to take me straight-away to Marrakech. I'm weary from the long plane trip from California, and gaze out the car window as we pass McDonalds and KFC and other too familiar touchstones of the West....the city seems more like Burbank than the other way around.

Three hours later I check into the Sofitel Marrakech Hotel. In the lobby a combo is playing, appropriately, "Strangers in the Night." A greeter sprinkles my hands with orange-flower water from a silver ewer. I drop my bags in the room, and decide to take a short walk. The air is languid and balmy, the buildings bathed in black. The Berbers, who called themselves Imazighen, "the free people," were the first to travel here, setting up a camp and market. (The English 'Berber' comes from the Arabic *barbar*, which itself is an adaptation of the Latin *barbarous* or 'barbarian— that is, one who did not speak Latin. The Arabs borrowed the word and used it to signify 'uncivilized' people; i.e., those who did not speak Arabic.) It was, for a long time, quite the insult. But today, here in Morocco, there is a re-consideration, and even a celebration, of the term, part of something called The Berber Pride movement.

After the arrival of Islam Marrakech was called, "The pearl that Allah threw over the Atlas Mountains." Nomads, though, called it The Red City, or The Ochre City, for the color of its walls and buildings, especially in the late afternoon pink light, but I've missed that golden hour.

The city was founded more than a thousand years ago by a tribe of warrior monks who carved out an empire from Algiers to Spain. In 1062 the Almoravid sultan Abou Bekr built the first palace and the first mosque near a water source, at the foot of the Gueliz hill. Here starts a story full of swirls and dips, a story of a city that will several times be capital of an empire, several times abandoned, nearly destroyed, renovated, re-installed, with the ebb and flow through Kasbah doors.

It is Marrakouch, the country of the sons of Kouch, in other words, the domain of the black warriors who came from Mauritania to support the Almoravid kings. It is the most Berber and the most African of the Imperial Cities of Morocco, and for a long time the richest. In its bones can be found a thousand years of history, from the scarce remnants of the first Almoravid magnificence to the blood of many battles.

With the day I hook up with Hamza Bouzouzou, an English teacher who became a guide four years ago, and ask him how he defines a Kasbah. He says it is a fortified village, an oasis on the trade route.

"It was dangerous to travel at night…it was a safe haven for travelers. It is the architecture of the nomad notion that 'the stranger is a friend.' Jews have been living here for 3000 years, and they often lived in the Kasbahs. The Arabs came 1400 years ago, and mixed with the Berbers. This has been a melting spot since the Phoenicians and the Romans, and it continues today. Everybody finds what they are looking for here. The Kasbah is a place where everybody feels secure, and enjoys one another's company. The Moroccans love new ideas; new adventures."

"Is there a modern Kasbah?"

"Morocco has to pass beneath your feet. Then you'll find out," he grins a scimitar.

With Mohammed at the wheel we slalom a wide boulevard busy with motor scooters and old Mercedes taxis. The edges are lined with date palms and jacaranda trees, all bright purple blossom and no leaves. We trundle by the red adobe walls of the city, six-feet thick, thirty-feet high, and pocked with random holes. Islamic tradition says that only Allah can make a perfect object. So, every time man makes something, it has to have some kind of flaw. Thus, each time Muslims build a wall or a Kasbah, it must have some kinds of physical imperfection, such as these holes. There is also the theory that these were 12th century scaffolding holes, or that they serve as a sophisticated medieval air conditioning system. The holes are also busy condos for birds, and Hitchcock supposedly found his inspiration for his film, *The Birds*, while watching one of these pocked walls from his Marrakech Hotel.

We ease through traffic past orange blossoms and hibiscus, over to the nerve center of the city, the dusty Vanity Fair known as Jemaa El F'na square. Of course it is not in any way shaped like a square (it is more like a crushed and bent rhomboid), but it is from this open mandala that the souks radiate. We park just beyond its borders, as within no cars are allowed. It was once a bus station, and featured in the Alfred Hitchcock film, *The Man Who Knew Too Much* (with James Stewart and Doris Day) as such...the opening murder takes place here. Before that it was a place of public executions, where heads of criminals were lopped off and placed on stakes, up until the early 20th century. The spectacles remain lurid and exotic, though less gory. It is the convention hall, wide umbrellas delineating booths, for small merchants, fortune tellers, musicians, water sellers (in signature jangling wide hats), snake charmers, monkey masters and mad men, both those who excel in the art of selling, and those who have lost their minds, and in either case I think I qualify for all-access-badge status. We pass orange juice barrows, henna tattoo makers, places where we can eat grilled meat, spikes and snails. Bikes and horse-drawn carriages and carts slide by; scooters buzz, often steered by young women wrapped in *hijabs*, head-scarves the devout wear as an affirmation of identity and modesty. They often cross paths with their sisters in high heels and tailored suits. Some of the men in long *jalabas* sport starched white shirts and ties showing at the neck; others have the pointed yellow leather slippers right out of the Arabian Nights showing below the hem.

Most of all, this place is a gathering of people of all sorts, a giant coffee shop…tourists (almost all of whom are wrapped in sunglasses), locals (most of whom are not, though many of the women shade with veils), salesmen, shoppers, and people from all over Africa and the world. For many here the rub and rancor of multiculturalism manifests itself in a kind of easy tolerance, even within the official bounds of religion and tradition. A saying here goes: "Nothing is true; all is permissible."

Rising above us, just beyond the square, is the pink-stoned, 253'-high Koutoubia minaret, built by the Almohads at the end of the 12th century, and a twin tower to the Giralda in Seville. It is, Hamza says, an example of Hispanic-Arabic architecture, topped with four golden balls of decreasing size, symbolizing the sun, the moon and the stars. The orbs were allegedly made from the melted down jewelry of Sultan Yacoub el Mansour's wife, in penance for her having eaten three grapes during Ramadan.

The minaret's name comes from a book market (Koutoub) that once thrived at its base, but is now gone, a fate perhaps similar to our own mega-chain bookstores. The site of the mosque is itself historic, having been originally occupied by a late 11th-century Kasbah, the Almoravid Dar el Hajar (House of Stone). The victorious Almohads destroyed much of the Almoravid city they found. In 1147 they built a large mosque, close to the Dar el Hajar fortress. This they had to do, as no Almohad would pray in a building put up by the heretic Almoravids. Unfortunately, the orientation of the new Almohad mosque was not quite right – the focal point in a mosque, indicated by the *mihrab*, or prayer niche, should be in the direction of Mecca, and it was discovered to be off. The solution was to build a second mosque – the present Koutoubia – even though the faithful at prayer could correct the directional problem themselves, under the direction of the imam. And there is also a white *koubba*, the Tomb of Lalla Zohra, the daughter of a freed slave who, as legend has, transformed into a dove each night.

Just to the north of the square we duck through a scalloped doorway, a *bab* in Arabic, into the mottled and crooked alleyways of the medina. It's like stepping through a time tunnel, into an ancient oriental chiaroscuro. The low-watt florescence lights, the sweet edgy smells, the greetings with hands so dry they feel like crushed autumn leaves. These arteries pulse with conversation and commerce. I yield to so many brilliant sights that my eyes, accustomed to copy-cat shopping malls, jam and overload.

"Dark, fierce and fanatical are these narrow souks of Marrakech," Edith Wharton wrote in 1919. "Marrakech is the great market of the south…not only the Atlas with its feudal chiefs and their wild clansman, but all that lies beyond of heat and savagery: the Sahara of the veiled Touaregs, Dakka, Timbuctoo, Senegal and the Soudan."

We find our way to the olive market, where casts and bowls and pyramids of the black and green fruit of *Olea europaea* tempt a taste, or the urge to knock something over, which I almost do when a vendor invites me to duck under his shelf to enter his stall and look around. It's all organic and local here, with more variety than Whole Foods (and considerably better prices).

The medina has a striking sense of fractured space, time and culture. All is motion….walking, buying, selling, exchanging. The canyons and couloirs are so packed with people, animals and objects that one has to learn a new way to navigate. Those who live or trade here don't so much walk as glide, ready at an instant to dodge to the right or left to avoid a pile of oncoming hides, a blind beggar, or a cart erupting with produce.

We pass the shoe market, where hundreds of shoes hang from the ceilings on strings; the purse market, hanging by purse strings; the music mart, where the rich interdental consonants of Arabic songs consume the air; the basket bazaar; a merchant unfurling a yo-yo. In the copper souk we watch the metal worked by craftsmen tapping with their legs crossed, faces set in vital concentration. The Laghzal Souk is home to the wool merchants. The el Btana to the sheepskin sellers. These are the works of Adam, the Arabic word for human, who was created by the divine craftsman, Allah. But over there is Eve…In one stall veiled women press around the stacks of underwear stalls, fingering lace and frilly wear. I can't tell their age for their coverage…they might be teens or middle-aged or septuagenarians, or some combination. At another stand there are racks of colored cell phones for sale, but nobody seems to be buying.

The spice market is a must-smell. The atmosphere is thick with scents that battle each other in the nose—the sharp sour smoke of tobacco, the perfumes of spices and teas. It is a mélange of snaking Arabic sounds and old scents: the tang of saffron, cumin, black pepper, ginger, verbena, cloves and orange flower. Among sacks of salted almonds, ground nuts and chick peas are piled high like mountains, alongside baskets of dates, and, on the apothecaries' shelves, pots of henna, vials of ghassoul clay (used as a traditional beauty treatment), flasks of rose extract, jasmine, mint, kohl, pieces of amber and smalls bottles of something called argan oil.

We wind about beneath a trellis-work of reeds and fall into the black magic market, where dried lizards, pythons, crocodiles, turtles, hedgehogs, lynx and unidentifiable creatures are chopped and minced and mixed with indecipherable spices to create elixirs, nostrums and potions to cast spells, to aid in fertility and virility, and here even cure intolerance. Hamza shows me a chunk of resin from a tree in the Sahara called *um nnass*, which he says women use to make their husbands love them more, by burning as in incense or mixing into a drink "without the other person even knowing."

In the Zarbia souk men in flowing *jalabas* hawk carpets, pouffes, *babouches* (the popular heelless leather slippers) and brocades. I get lost among the cornucopias of chotkies and tat, and am somehow spilled back out to the main Jemaa El F'na Square, where one *charmeurs de serpent* pulls me under his black umbrella and wags his head at his Egyptian Cobra (actually, *Naja haje legionis,* a sub-species found in southern Morocco) as his associate blows his bagpipe-like melody in his *ghaita*. The big black snake promptly flares its hood and snaps the embroidered beige skull cap off the charmer's head, as the flute-like instrument flutters in the background, and a goat-skin hand-drum pounds...pam,pam,pam-pam-pam. Then of course, he wraps the snake around my neck, and lets it flick its tongue at mine as though a kiss....it is drama, and worth a tip.

Location, location, location....the gift of geography gave Morocco its multiculturalism. Lapped by the trade routes of three seas—the Atlantic, the Mediterranean, and the Sahara—here washes the goods, the economics and influences from three continents: Europe, Asia and Africa. To Morocco, the world was flat long before Tom Friedman.

I stumble through a heavy carved wooden door studded with big iron nails and bolts, the hinges, Hamza tells me, a rendering of the five fingers of Fatima. In Morocco the Hand of Fatima is a popular women's talisman (from Arabic *tilsamen* "to make marks like a magician"), and ranges from literal representations of a hand to highly abstract designs containing a pattern in five units, for her five fingers. The Hand of Fatima is said to protect brides, pregnant women and newborn children, considered especially vulnerable. Fatima brings healing and compassion, for individuals and nations alike, and helps in achieving forgiveness and understanding.

On the other side of the door I have fallen into a secret place, a *riad* (which means "garden," but has come to represent houses with courtyards and foundations that have been turned into inns) just a membrane from the clamor of the medina, and am wowed by the contrast. It is the tradition in these parts that beauty should be veiled. The houses of Marrakech are all turned inward; no windows look to the street. To the outside world they present a blank wall, an anonymous door. To their inhabitants they offer fountained courtyards, gorgeous tile work, deep divans, shade, internal peace, and four symmetrical flower beds utterly cloistered from the outside world.

The Koran depicts paradise as four gardens, interpreted as four stages through which the seeker travels on his inward journey toward God. "A garden enclosed is my sister, my spouse; a spring shut up, a fountain sealed" says the Song of Solomon. Many Muslims have taken the holy writings to mean that the veil is an extension of this cloistered space, that the woman, seeing but unseen behind it, moves through teeming life as if sequestered in her own garden.

As the day slips into the evening the square loads with more activity, from acrobats to tooth pullers, healers to hustlers, fortune tellers and storytellers. The tales are tall here...as a local saying goes, "If you're going to tell the truth, you better have one foot in the stirrup."

In one eddy of the square I watch an ensemble of barefooted leaping, spinning Gnawa musicians in their white garments and twirling tasseled caps. Gnawa refers to an ethnic group- religious order descended from former slaves from Sub-Saharan Africa, who marched in caravans that stopped in the Kasbahs on the trade route north, some of whom stayed and assimilated. The last slave caravan, it is said, crossed the Sahara in the 1950s.

The name appears to originate from the Saharan Berber dialect word *aguinaw*, meaning "black (men)". This word in turn may be derived from the name of a city significant in the 11th century, in what is now western Mali, called *Gana*, in Arabic *Ghana* or *Jenna* and in Portuguese and later French *Guinea* or *Jenné*.

Popular history credits the Moroccan Sultan Ahmed Al Mansour Ad-Dahbi's conquest in 1591 of part of the Songhai Empire, in particular Timbuktu, with bringing large numbers of captives and slaves back across the Sahara to form the Gnawa.

While adopting Islam Gnawa continued to celebrate ritual possession devoted to dances of fright. The rite of possession is called *Derdba* and proceeds through the night, animated jointly by a master musician (*maâlem*) accompanied by his troupe. Gnawa music mixes classical Islamic Sufism with pre-Islamic African traditions.

A few years ago I produced a project that traced the American Blues trail backwards from Chicago down the Mississippi to New Orleans. It was there I heard the theory that the blues traces back through the Diaspora back to Africa, back to the Gnawa.

In Moroccan popular culture, Gnawas, through their ceremonies, are considered to be experts in the magical treatment of scorpion stings and psychic disorders. They can evoke ancestral saints. They heal diseases and drive out evil through dance, sound, colors, imagery, perfumes and fright.

I stand in a trance watching the Gnawans play their deeply hypnotic music, marked by low-toned, urgent rhythmic sintir melodies, call and response singing, hand clapping and the shaking of rattle-like cymbals called *krakeb*. How do they do that voodoo? It's a scene from which I don't want to awaken.

A number of Western musicians have drawn upon and collaborated with Gnawa musicians, from Robert Plant and Jimmy Page, and my favorite since college days, Randy Weston, who for years lived in Tangier. I had always hoped to meet Randy, if just to lend a word of appreciation.

5. THE ARGANAUTS

"Examine what is said, not him who speaks."
–Moroccan proverb

I awake to a cascade of chanting calls leaping from mosque to mosque, music that moves like the waters of courtyard fountains. As the prayers, in tones of ineffable yearning, exhort those who hearken that it is better to pray than to sleep, roosters begin to crow. The chanting seems to magically create the new day.

Hamza is a font of knowledge, a river of words. After breakfast he tells me I should see the Kasbah in Essaouira, which will help illustrate the concept, he contends. And he offers to escort me, west to the coast. The drive is a desolate grumble, through a dry land. But there is a spidery tree with a short, gnarled trunk and holly-green leaves that we see in ever larger numbers…some even harbor goats that have climbed into the branches and are munching the thorny leaves. "Flying goats," Mohammed the driver calls them. He says the trees are argans, the Berber gold, exclusive to this region of southwest Morocco.

We pull over at a wide spot in the road called Tidzi, and steer into the walls of the Coopérative Ajddigue ("argan blossom"), a woman's collective that produces and distributes Argan, promoted as "the miracle oil." Hamza says, "The future of Morocco is its past, and reviving its traditions….and this is proof."

Outside the compound bamboo blankets are spread over the ground with argan nuts drying in the sun. Through a dark doorway comes an arrhythmic beat that sounds like Moroccan maracas gone wild. The source: a half-dozen Berber women in *ktibs*, traditional head scarves, squatting against the walls in a long room of Amish simplicity. They are cracking the oblong fruit with sharp stones, and sorting the shells and the nuts in metal pans and colorful baskets. It takes about 70 pounds of nuts to create one quart of the oil, about two-day's labor. It's not all work, though, as the women swill the nectar of gossip and enjoy the company of friends outside the home. Some walk long distances to come here, and consider it a second home.

In an adjacent room a head-dressed woman feeds the shucked nuts into a pair of metal blenders, which then ooze out the oil. And of course there is a little shop where visitors can buy their miracle oil, not just for its qualities but because it is helping to make life better for these women.

I sit and crack a few nuts to get the feeling of this work, and must admit there is something vital and satisfying about using hands and rocks and human power…nothing electric…to unearth a little treasure. I then buy a bottle of the cooking oil, and dip a piece of pita into the liquid, which is slightly darker yet thinner than olive oil. It has a hazelnut taste; there is a faintly erotic buzz. Baba Mina, the vice-president of these Arganauts, says the nut has been used for hundreds of years as a food source—it is high in vitamin E, antioxidants and essential fatty acids. But recently new uses have emerged: It is now an anti-wrinkle cream, supposedly moisturizing and making the skin supple (and it's true that these women have smooth skin); it strengthens nails, and can turn dry hair smooth and shiny. It is becoming a popular massage oil. Some use it as baby oil. Traditionally it was used as a cure for chickenpox, acne and rheumatism, but Baba Mina says it is now even used to treat cancer. Like olive oil, it is recommended for its anti-cholesterol properties. It is used in salads, soups, tajines and couscous, even for frying eggs. And, of course, it is an aphrodisiac. "It is important that foreigners buy argan, "Baba Mina says, "as it makes these cooperatives possible." No twig goes unused. Beyond what foreigners buy and employ, a pressed cake from the shells is used to feed cattle; the wood is used for furniture; and the pulp is used to feed goats. Goats, Hamza says, have a craving for the seed, though their stomachs can't crack its hard casing if swallowed uncrunched. Enterprising Moroccans recover the whole seeds from goats' droppings, and sell them as the premium version, just like Kopi Luwak, the undigested coffee beans that are shat by Sumatran civet cats and then sold in the West for up to $600 a pound.

What makes this all unusual and exciting is that Morocco is primarily an Arab culture, and in much of the Arab world women are not permitted to work, sometimes not even to leave the home. But here the King has endorsed these cooperatives, and the work not only gives the women a measure of economic freedom, but also a sense of identity, of comradeship, and pride. And Baba Mina says even the husbands are pleased, as the wives no longer have to ask them for money to go shopping…they have their own. It has created a new kind of tolerance between the sexes. "It's the miracle oil," she asserts, "because it is a miracle these women are now working and owning their own lives."

Plus, it turns out this initiative is good for the continuation of a culture—and for the environment. The localized economics help to halt the rural exodus. The trees were traditionally cut as firewood and to make charcoal, and for a time it looked as though they might be cut to oblivion. In less than a decade more than a third of the argan forest had disappeared. But with the new economics the argans are worth more in the ground, and are proliferating. And it turns out their profuse roots seek out water even in high temperatures, and stabilize the soil and fight erosion, doing a part to keep the advancing Sahara desert at bay.

Back in the car we thunder the open country, and rise over a small hill to see the sheen of the Atlantic. During the mega-continent epoch of Gondwanaland this part of Morocco was attached to Pennsylvania. Now some 3,600 miles separates the shores.

6. NOSTALGIA FOR THE FUTURE

*"There is only one certain castle I know of where it is good to be locked in.
Better to die than to give back the key. It is Mogador in Africa."*
–Paul Claudel, *Satin Slipper*

We wind down a narrow road into Essaouira, to the sound of
gulls squawking and children rollicking. We park, and I step over
dunes thick with marram grass, and down to the line where light
sand meets the dark. Here at my feet is bahr-al-zhulumat, the Sea
of Darkness, as the Arabs once called the Atlantic. When Uqba
bin Nafi, the 7th century Arab general who set out to conquer
North Africa, reached the bahr-al-zhulumat, he crashed into the
thrashing surf and pointed his sword to the west. Neither he nor
anyone with him knew what lay beyond. Morocco would later
become known to the Arabs as al-Maghreb, the Land of Sunset.

With mechanical regularity waves are washing at my feet.
Out towards the horizon, little boats are nodding inshore to
provide freshly caught sardines for the lunchtime tajines; beyond
a set of purple islands float like clouds. These are the Iles
Purpuraires, where Romans in the first century traded for a
precious purple dye for their royal robes, the dye secreted by
murex, a type of mollusk that thrives off these motes. Cleopatra
loved the stuff so much that she dyed the sails of her royal barge
purple to meet Marc Antony. Times change, and so do styles. A

couple generations later wearing the color purple could be a crime of fashion. Cleopatra's grandson, Ptolemy, was murdered by Emperor Caligula for having the cheekiness to sport a purple robe.

The vivid, fade-resistant pigment was never successfully produced commercially, and the undisclosed extraction techniques were assumed lost in the siege of Constantinople in 1453. But here in Essaouira the colorant is still available in several shops, for the right price.

The islands, where most of the Roman relics have long been excavated, are now a reserve for a dying species of bird, Eleonora's Falcon. Pre-ecology gourmets speak greedily of mouthwatering omelets made from the falcon's eggs. (Each egg alone is now worth as much as $100,000 on the black market.) The island's first guard would treat himself to one of these omelets each morning for breakfast. The scattered eggshells finally gave him away. He was chucked into the sea, and after he was fished out, replaced. The island was closed for some time, but can now be visited with a special permit.

Essaouira's narrative reaches back nearly 3000 years, when seafaring Phoenicians first came calling. Its original name was Tassort, which refers to its Kasbah and it fortress-like walls. Its name is derived from Tashelhit, the southern Souss Berber language. In Moroccan Arabic, it's called Saouira, which literally means 'picture.' "Show me that precious picture," the sultan is supposed to have said while examining the plans for the new town. For a long time Essaouira was the outlet for Timbuktu, sending ostrich feathers, salt, spices, and gold dust through its harbor; and bringing in silk and perfumes.

In the 7th century the Phoenicians dubbed this port Migdal, a word for 'watchtower.' The Portuguese were only able to hold onto the port from 1506 to 1510, because the surrounding Berber tribes came together under Arab leadership to defeat them. The Portuguese called this region Mogador, a distant cousin to Migdal, and a name still used today.

The city then changed hands again when Sidi Mohammed Ben Abdellah had the Essaouira medina designed to bring great commerce to this region of Morocco. Thousands of Moroccan Jews came to the region for commerce and stayed until most of them departed for Israel in the mid-1900s. Within the Kasbah there is a synagogue and church, and Stars of David are carved over doors marking the homes where the Jewish merchants once lived. Blue-headed sparrows flit about the courtyards, bringing good luck, say the locals.

Two hundred years ago Essaouira had the largest Jewish population in the Muslim world, almost half the town's population. For a time this city had more synagogues than mosques. And it was here in 1941 that Andre Azoulay was born, who is today a senior advisor to King Mohammed VI, the only Jewish counselor to a modern Arab leader. In fact, the first Jew elected to the U.S. Senate was Florida Democrat David Levy Yulee, in 1845, and his family had come from Essaouira.

Artistry in this town is an organ, like the heart, and to remove it would kill the host. It was for many years a kind of hippie haven.

Bob Marley and Cat Stevens made pilgrimages here. Legend has it that Jimi Hendrix was attracted to its mystical qualities and tried purchasing the entire nearby village of Diabat, and the Portuguese ruins led him to write his song "Castles in the Sand." There is truth in ruins, but not in this case. In truth Hendrix wrote the song well before his long summer weekend in 1969 in Essaouira, but the artistic license fits right in.

Essaouira's medina has a worn-in appearance, old but light. The Portuguese influence imbues, with light brown stone and white houses with crisp blue shutters. The so-called Portuguese fort, a ruined watchtower, stands guard at the far end of the beach, an eerie pile of stones beaten by the waves and wind. At a small fortified zone overlooking the port spread the canons of Essaouira. Orson Wells picked this spot for key outside shots when he filmed *Othello* here in 1949; it cursed the production with its winds, and even now as I stand in Shakespearean pose it whips up a powerful thirst.

I quench my thirst at the Orson Welles bar in the l'Hôtel des Îles, and then head out to walk the windy narrow streets of the town, between the cool blue and whitewashed walls, beneath a blizzard of seagulls. The air rings with the talk of merchants in striped *burnooses*; of fishmongers lording over stalls of silver fish. Artisanal crafts are everywhere, especially pieces made from the area's thuya wood, inlaid with delicate marquetry of ebony, mother of pearl and silver thread. I wouldn't mind being wrecked on the shoals of this town, and here then set about to finishing my unfinished novel.

With evening I am visited by Chakib El Mokhtar Ghadouani from the Département Presse of the Office National Marocain du Tourisme, who is here to check up on me, but also to take me to dinner at one of Marrakech's finest, Dar Marjana. "He who does not share his food is not one of us," Chakib quotes the Koran as we walk from the car across a busy street. The entrance is modest, more like a doorway to a cheap boutique, but the inside is a posh and exclusive eatery. Chakib says that the good restaurants here are like Moroccan philosophy—the beauty is on the inside. It is an intimate palace of arches, low banquettes and cushions, old tiles, painted doors, candlelight, and immense brass trays.

Chakib is a delight, and is not only a student of the cultures and landscapes of Morocco, but also a video game nut, like my son Walker. I order a bottle of Domaine de Sahara, vin Rouge du Maroc. With much ceremony the waiter decants a tasting splash into my glass. I swill the wine around in my glass, then around my mouth, and nod to the waiter. He pours us each half glasses, and I lift the stem of mine between my thumb and forefinger and propose a toast to Morocco. But Chakib raises his palm and says no. He doesn't drink, he says, but he does play Prince of Persia, Guitar Hero and Pro Evolution Soccer on his Playstation 3.

As I sip the splendid wine my attention is drawn to a Gnawa performer, who twirls the tassel on his hat like a helicopter while he plucks his *gembri,* a three-stringed guitar. Then out pops a belly-dancer, a baffling Egyptian import that seems utterly at odds with the Gnawan soundtrack. But before we can stuff any dirhams into the spangly, wriggling bodice, the food begins to arrive. Huge beautifully arranged platters are presented on the round, knee-high table, from fresh salads drizzled with argan oil, couscous covered with foi gras, to a clay conical tajine covering a sizzling sea bass, ending with a cinnamon pastille so ethereal it is like eating cloud. High caloric Moroccan meals are a legacy of when meals were prepared to sustain laborers in the fields. I wonder, though, if Chakib is fattening me up for the following day. "Morocco is a great melting pot of food and culture," Chakib offers up. "And the Kasbah was the great tajine of cultures."

"What is the modern equivalent of the ancient Kasbah?' I ask Chakib between courses. He looks at me, mapping my face. "You'll see," he intones with a faintly sardonic end note.

7. LA VIE EN ROSE

"Take me down little Susie, take me down,
I know you think you're the queen of the underground,
And you can send me dead flowers every morning, Send me dead flowers
by the US mail, Say it with dead flowers in my wedding, And I won't
forget to put roses on your grave.
No, I won't forget to put roses on your grave."
–Mick Jagger/Keith Richards, 1971

Night hangs in the air by a thread with the muezzin's first crackling wail for prayer. We slurp some café noir topped with milk at the hotel restaurant, and set out to drive over the glow of the Atlas Mountains, rising now above the red walls of the city. It is a sight said to have moved men to tears, though in my case it may be the tajine from the night before.

We coil up over the Tizi n' Tichka Pass, as I had on my last visit with Walker, only this time the weather is spectacular, and so I sit back and enjoy the scenery and the ride. Little terraced fields cling to steep hillsides; small watermills turn grinding corn. Cubed houses crouch on bare hills; there is no presumption in them. There are many Kasbahs along the way, some troglodytic and tucked away on stony ledges from which they were quarried. One we miss is Sir Richard Branson's retreat, Kasbah Tamadot. In 1998 when Branson set off from Marrakech on his round-the-world balloon attempt, his mother, Eve Branson, discovered this

Kasbah, and convinced her son to buy it and turn it into a high-end eco-resort....so high-end it is beyond my means, though I vow that if I win the lottery I will give it try.

This is indeed one of the great drives of the world. According to Moroccan lore, Atlas was a Greek god living in the Mediterranean. He was a Titan, busy fighting other giants. One day he lost a battle and decided to hide along the African shoreline. He was so gigantic, of course, that when he lay down to sleep his head was tucked into Tunisia and his feet stretched all the way down to Marrakech. The position was so nice that he never woke up again, and became a mountain range. Snow fell on the Atlas regularly, for a few months of the year, but he could always feel his feet happily ensconced in the desert.

The road twists like a length of gray ribbon wrapped round the red earth of the mountainside. We pass through what feels like half-a-dozen different countries in the space of a couple of hours. Agricultural flatlands give way to arid mountains. We spiral above olive groves, fruit orchards and bamboo fields; above cool oases and sun-baked Kasbahs against cliffs traced with feathery waterfalls and tall shadows. The snow seen on distant peaks from Marrakesh is now close enough to touch. The high Atlas has more than 400 peaks over 10,000 feet, and many are snow-covered year round. Chakib points out various landmarks, but it's difficult to hear over the screech of scenery.

We bridge the top of the pass at 7414' above sea level, the highest road in Morocco, and unwind towards the Sahara. Pine trees are soon replaced by acacias and tamarinds. Colors shift constantly across a spectrum that ranges from charcoal to crimson. Soon the landscape is devoid of vegetation. The pale stone settlements that cling to the sides are coated in dust, their sharp-edged geometry describing misleading perspectives among the sensually carved stones. And then the road oozes like a wound out of the Atlas.

But then we turn towards color....we motor for about an hour alongside the southern edge of the Atlas, over to El Kelaa-des-M'Gouna, in the Dades Valley (sometimes called the Valley of the Roses), where we stop to smell the prickly-stemmed, pinnate-leaved, showy-flowered shrubs of the genus *Rosa* ...we have trundled into the 46th annual Rose Festival (with the trendy theme this year of 'sustainable development').

My eyes water as though passing someone with too much aftershave as we steer through the town. Two huge distilling plants that create most of the rose water found in Moroccan foods and its perfumes are working overtime this week. Once a year, in May, this town throws a party to celebrate the harvests, and we soak it in. It is a sort of African Pasadena during the Rose Bowl, as there are dancing, drumming, singing, and a parade of floats, all adorned with flowers the colors of strawberries.

From the loudspeakers blares a heavy music, a sort of 'Maroc & Roll,' and in the main arena a group of men in striped *jalabas* pound cactus drums while women in long-white dresses and red scarves sway and keen and ululate. Then out steps a couple, the local version of John Travolta and Olivia Newton-John, who prance on Berber rugs and flutter their shoulders like butterflies.

When the music stops, the ceremony begins, and on stage a young girl is crowned Miss Rose, her black hair coiffed as at a prom, her hands richly hennaed, her chest adorned with a huge yellow necklace of gourds, and her head crowned with a an elaborate headdress looped with colored yarn (but no roses).

Around 2,500 tons of blossoms are harvested each year, deftly picked by women and children in the early morning. We try to stop into one of the French-owned processing shops, the Biolandes distillation plant, but the manager is not suffering from an overdose of hospitality, and shoos us away. So we head down the road to an artisan coop, and there, in one of the 30 shops, we watch as a man shows us how he forges a curved silver dagger, and pounds the designs of roses in the camel bone handles, a craft the Jews once mastered, but most left from here for Israel in 1967, and now the craft is carried on by a group of Muslims. Goethe said that a requisite for contented living was "Patience enough to toil until some good is accomplished." It takes three to five days to forge and craft one of these daggers.

We drive outside of town a short ways, metal to the petals, and stop by what appears to be a pointillist painting. It is, rather, a field of pink roses, adjacent to a Kasbah of similar hue. Roses grow like weeds here, and the perfume is heady and heavy, sweet in the dry desert air. No sense memory is stronger, nor more intensely personal, than the olfactory kind, some scientists claim. I now read newspapers from my Kindle, but the device doesn't work here, so when I pick up a copy of *Morocco Today*, and bury my nose in it, there is a cologne-like rush. The faint oily notes, vaguely shoe-polish-ish, in the printer's ink, mingled with the musty scent of paper. It conjures up my time as a paperboy, bundling and delivering *The Washington Post* in the predawn darkness.

But lifting my nose from the paper, an unforgettable and all pervasive fragrance wafts. Its roots date back over a thousand years to when pilgrims first passed through Persia and plucked the roses they then brought here. It's an example of a culture as an open garden that assimilates the best of what it encounters, and plants the seeds that nourish the soul.

Here I meet a young big-eyed woman named Fatima-Zohra El Haqaoui, dressed in white save for a rose-colored wrap, who is picking the five-petaled roses, celebrating her engagement. She dips her eyes, and places her right hand on her heart. She has me at "Merhaba."

She invites me to the rooftop of the nearby Kasbah for some hot mint tea. She leads me to a set of extremely high and steep stairs…I can barely stretch my considerable legs to make each rise, and Fatima needs to use her hands, as though rock climbing. "Why are the steps so high?" I ask

"Berber child proofing…it keeps the kids from the rooftop."

We make the summit, stretched and exhausted, and sit on a wool carpet beneath a canopy of tamarisk, where we sip from golden cups in the shadow of the Atlas Mountains. Fatima recites a throaty Berber poem between servings, which seems some sort of lawful magic. "*Sihr halal*" is what the Arabs call the effect their poetry produces on its hearers. The magic was born in the desert, among the Bedouin of pre-Islamic Morocco, who, though illiterate, were among the most accomplished poets of any age.

I ask her what makes the roses here so special, and she tells me that legend has it that Mohammed put a drop of sweat from his brow into a bottle as he ascended to heaven. His grandson then by mistake broke the bottle while in Isfahan, and from the prophetable liquid sprang the roses that ultimately made their way here.

Fatima, Chakib and I take a quick lunch (in Morocco, a fast-food experience is something less than the time for a round of golf) at the Hotel Rose MGoun, where the receptionist sprinkles us liberally with rose water. A few hours later, sated in all the senses, I make my way back to the car. I stoop inside to a sultry, intoxicating perfume, so silken as to seem illicit. Mohammed, my driver, has strewn fresh roses all over the dashboard of his black Toyota. What a gift this place offers. The west may have invented nuclear power, SUVs and deep-fried Twinkies, but Morocco has its roses.

8. HOLLYWEIRD

"Reality is merely an illusion, albeit a persistent one."
– Albert Einstein, 1949

For a place to bed for the night Mohammed points the car to Ouarzazate, the former French Foreign Legion garrison, founded in 1928. This is the town where my trek ended a few years ago. It has changed a bit, with its heightened status as a movie set…classics such as *Cleopatra*, *The Man Who Would Be King*, *The Last Temptation of Christ*, and *Lawrence of Arabia* were limned here, as well as more recent fare, such as *Gladiator* and *Babel*. Martin Scorsese even filmed *Kundun* here, and somehow managed to make southern Morocco look like Tibet (fooled me). There are two movie studios here now, and a Museum of Cinema, which all seems like illusion turned on its head, as we are in an amazing landscape that doubles for Hollywood. It reminds of the disenchantment I had when I went to my first movie as a child, *The Blob* with Steve McQueen, and the usher tore my ticket in half…I felt like I had stumbled into a place where I was being reprimanded in the dark.

We check into Le Berbère Palace, a grand hotel with the traditional architectural style of a Kasbah, but filled with props and costumes from films shot nearby, including life-size statues from the movie Cleopatra. I half expect Charles Boyer to utter "Come weez me to the Kasbah," as he allegedly did (as the character Pepe Le Moko) to Hedy Lamarr in the movie *Algiers*. But that classic line, too, is an illusion. The phrase was not in the movie, but rather uttered by Pepe Le Peuw, a parody of Boyer's character, in a 1949 cartoon.

This could be The Beverly Hills Hotel. It's slow season, so I am promised a special room at no extra charge. It turns out to be a lovely suite, and my bellman says it is where Leonardo diCaprio stayed recently while filming *Body of Lies*. As he drops my bag and waits for a tip he catalogues others who have enjoyed this special room: Halle Berry, Timothy Dalton, Michael Douglas, Anthony Quinn, Ben Kingsley, Jean-Claude Van Damme, Omar Sharif, Russell Crowe, Richard Harris, Gerard Depardieu, Brad Pitt with Angelina Jolie, and Orlando Bloom. As he counts the dirhams I place in his hand, which I consider a healthy tip, he looks back up at me in disappointment, condemning me to lesser stardom. So, I reach deeper in my pocket, and insure my handprints in his mental walk of fame.

Lying where three rivers converge, Ouarzazate is a natural crossroads linking east with west and north with south. Until coastal shipping came to Morocco in the late 19th-century it was a busy stopping-off point for the caravans that plied the trans-Saharan trade route. Thousands of camels and their owners made the arduous 1100-mile, 52-day journey across the Sahara to Timbuktu, bearing cargoes of salt, dates, barley and goatskins, and returning with the gold, slaves, indigo and the ivory that would make North Africa wealthy.

In the bath of morning sunlight we head over to the nearby Kasbah Taourirt, the once sumptuous residence of the Pasha of

Marrakech from 1918 to 1956. The structure encloses a small village, accessed by a network of alleys and gateways. The Kasbah houses the old apartments of the Glaoui family, who ruled southern Morocco and controlled access to the High Atlas for 200 years.

The Glaoui clan was one of wild men. It was said of T'Hami el Glaoui, the last Pasha, that he never pardoned, and never forgave. He was a falconer. He had "talent scouts" in France and throughout Morocco, agents positioned at railroad stations who pretended to be guides and procured for him fine European women. He was variously described as barbaric, intelligent, ambitious, insatiable, and generous with jewels. Winston Churchill said he admired him.

Gavin Maxwell wrote in his book, *Lords of the Atlas,* that "once the doors on the harem closed behind a new acquisition she knew that she would never again leave the women's quarters of her master until she was carried out to the cemetery. From then on she was a woman of the harem, her life bounded by its jealousies and rivalries and petty squabbles and household breakages that were judged and punished by the Glaoui himself; her conversation limited to the endless sexual gossip of her fellow concubines; her sexual life limited to her necessarily infrequent turn in her master's bed and the sometimes passionate solace of her own sex. She would never again see any other man than T'hami face to face." In the 1950s Pasha T'hami conspired with the French to deport King Muhammad V, who had been agitating for independence. The Pasha picked the wrong side. When he died in 1956 it was said he reappeared in the shape of a black cobra rising from his tomb.

The Kasbah's tightly packed houses and stately towers, made of a mixture of chalk and sand, melt almost imperceptibly into the surrounding ochre-blushed landscape. Like cubes of clay, the dwellings hide away from the implacable sun—a narrow doorway being the only connection with the outside world. Light and air come in through the central courtyard.

Our interpreter, Jawad Bizza, who says he has been guiding for 29 years, looks like a young Steven Segal in a beige baseball cap, and begins each sentence with "Believe you me…" He drops historical lore as copiously and freely as a man on a bench scattering cups of birdseed. He walks us upstairs, and points out how the glassless windows are near the floor in each room. He explains that the harem women sat on the floors and looked out the windows for entertainment; and also that circulation of cooler air is more effective with this low construction. The balconies were where women could call to each other, exchanging gossip and news. "The women's telephones," he calls them. Then Jawad motions to duck my head down, and follow him through an Alice In Wonderland-sized passageway to a large and ornate room. "This is the Pasha's domain, and he built the entrance so low so that any visitor had to bow to him." And as he points out the design patterns, which seem to freeze detail into a cult of itself. He offers that the architecture here, and throughout Morocco, is a fusion of styles from the various influencing religions and cultures, from Andalusian to Moorish, Christianity to Jewish, Berber to

Arab. "It's not about the clothes," Steven Segal says. "It's about what's inside." And he bows slightly while letting his right hand rest gently on his heart.

Wandering about this wild warren of a Kasbah it seems it might have been designed by Frank Gehry, the celebrity architect who long ago lost his plumb bob, and turned the scaffolding of sound into a museum with the Experience Music Project in Seattle, not far from where I lived for many years. Perhaps Gehry was inspired by the Kasbahs. One of his recent works, the Stata Center at the Massachusetts Institute of Technology, houses MIT's computer-science and philosophy departments behind a façade of bizarre angles and windows. But the building's most radical innovation is on the inside. The entire structure was conceived with the nomadic lifestyles of modern students and faculty in mind. It was conceived as a kind of "hybrid space," similar to what Moroccans employed for centuries.

The fact that people are no longer tied to specific places for functions such as studying or learning means that there is a drop in demand for traditional, private, enclosed spaces such as offices or classrooms, and simultaneously a rise in demand for semi-public spaces that can be informally appropriated to ad-hoc workspaces, just as Moroccans have always done. In the 20th century architecture was about specialized structures—offices for working, cafeterias for eating, and so forth. This was necessary because workers needed to be near things such as landline phones, fax machines and filing cabinets, and because the economics of building materials favored repetitive and simple structures, such as grid patterns for cubicles.

The new architecture makes spaces intentionally multifunctional, just as the inside of Kasbahs had rooms that combined for sleeping, cooking, socializing and meeting. This means that 21st-century aesthetics may be the opposite of the sci-fi chic that 20th-century futurists once imagined. Architects are instead thinking about light, air, trees and gardens, all in the service of human connections. Buildings will have much more varied shapes than before, just as no two Kasbahs are alike.

The future looks like the past in many ways, even in architecture. In the not too distant future there will be more "on-demand spaces" and "drop-in centers," with flexible layouts that facilitate collaboration. Nomadism may not be good for the office industry as such, but there are opportunities. Some developers are building offices that are more like community centers in which mobile workers come in, find all the services they might need—from tech support to copying—and satisfy their needs for "work, love and play" as well, with the aid of fitness studios, restaurants, cooking classes and music rooms. My old shop, Microsoft, based in Redmond, Washington, has done that with an office in Seattle that is filled with unassigned workstations...if the commute is bad, just pop over to the satellite, plug in to the corp net, and work from there.

The academic name for such spaces is "third places," a term originally coined by the sociologist Ray Oldenburg in his 1989 book, *The Great, Good Place*. At the time, long before mobile technologies became widespread, Mr. Oldenburg wanted to distinguish between the sociological functions of people's first places (their homes), their second places (offices) and the public spaces that serve as safe, neutral and informal meeting points. The Kasbahs were all three, but as western concepts of work/life balance evolved, these were separated.

A good third place makes admission free or cheap—the price of a cup of coffee, say—offers creature comforts, is within walking distance for a particular neighborhood and draws a group of regulars and strangers. Rick's Café Americain in the movie *Casablanca* is an example.

Mr. Oldenburg's thesis was that third places were in general decline. More and more people, especially in suburban societies such as America's, were moving only between their first and second places, making extra stops only at alienating and anonymous locations such as malls, which fail as third places. Society was at risk of coming unstuck without these venues for spreading ideas and forming bonds.

No sooner was the term coined than big business queued up to claim that it was building new third places. The most prominent was Starbucks, the chain of coffee houses that started in Seattle and is now hard to avoid anywhere (though not yet in Morocco). Starbucks admits that as it went global it lost its ambiance of a "home away from home". However, it also spotted a new opportunity in catering to nomads. Its branches offer not only sofas but also desks and newspaper racks. Bookshops such as Barnes & Noble are also offering more coffee and crumbs, as are churches, YMCAs and public libraries, all in some emulation of the Kasbah.

Starbucks, McDonald's, and their ilk all come up short against the café culture of Morocco, the original "third places." The traditional café in this part of the world is conceived of as a club where, in addition to enjoying the usual amenities of a café, a man may, if he wishes, eat, sleep, bathe and store his personal effects. The typical Moroccan comes to a café in order to participate as intensely as possible in the collective existence of his friends and neighbors, as well as the random passers-through, the nomads. The customers in these shops converse, tell stories, eat, smoke, sleep, and play games: cards, checkers, dominoes, Parcheesi and during Ramadan, bingo. But with its luxury of unmeasured time the Moroccan café is out of harmony with present western concepts.

So, do these western-style oases for nomads actually play the social role of third places? Many fear that cyber-nomads are "hollowing them out." It is becoming commonplace for a café to be full of people with headphones on, speaking on their cell phones or hunched over laptops hacking away at their keyboards, more engaged with their e-mail inbox than with the people touching their elbows. These places are physically inhabited but psychologically evacuated, which leaves people feeling more isolated than they would be if the café were merely empty. That is because the physical presence of other human beings is psychologically and neurologically arousing, but now produces no reward. Quite simply, we have not evolved biologically to be happy in these situations.

9. NO PLACE LIKE ROAM

"In place of a world, there is a city, a point, in which the whole life of broad regions is collecting while the rest dries up. In place of a type-true people, born of and grown on the soil, there is a new sort of nomad, cohering unstably in fluid masses, the parasitical city dweller, tradition-less, utterly matter-of-fact, religionless, clever, unfruitful, deeply contemptuous of the countryman and especially that highest form of countryman, the country gentleman."
–Oswald Spengler, 1926

The adventure travel company I co-founded, Mountain Travel Sobek, is based in Emeryville, California, adjacent to Oakland, where I lived for many years. My favorite haunt was Oakland's Nomad Café, which now regularly hosts live jazz and poetry readings, and actually turns off the Wi-Fi router at those times so that people mingle more. It is, in some ways, a kind of modern Kasbah.

Most nomads are quite open to this sort of thing. Technology aside, there is not such a big difference between a geek with earphones and a laptop today and a Tangier existentialist watching the world go by at the Café Hafa in the 1950s. The first might be simultaneously instant-messaging, listening to music and e-mailing, the other puffing a Gitane and jotting down notes about being and nothingness. But as soon as an attractive new customer breezes in, both will instantaneously realign their focus of interest.

As more third places pop up and spread, they also change entire cities. Just as buildings during the 20th century were specialized by function, towns were as well. Suburbs were for living, downtowns for working and other areas for playing. But urban nomadism makes districts, like buildings, multifunctional. Parts of town that were monocultures gradually become fine-grained mixed-use neighborhoods more akin in human terms to the many Moroccan pre-industrial villages than to modern western suburbs.

There is a simultaneous movement to "charismatic exurbs," such as Angels Camp in the foothills of the Sierras, where I lived for a decade when running Sobek. It was a community of nomads then as Sobek guides from around the world would pass through and crash on my couch. Now the new nomads are building "consensual communities" with lifestyles reminiscent of the Utopia movements of earlier times.

The same trend is also changing traffic patterns. In the US in 1986, before the era of mobility and at the dawn of the PC era (Microsoft went public in March of that year), the diurnal flow of the post-war commuting pattern prevailed, which had baby-boomers sitting in traffic jams at 8am and 5pm between the suburbs and the downtowns. In 1996 a new circumferential pattern began to emerge as jobs shifted to the suburbs, so the baby-boomers were now sitting in jams on the beltways. At the same time the fastest-growing group was telecommuters.

Things started looking very different after the millennium. Younger workers were now joining the baby-boomers in the workforce. Car trips had stopped increasing and were even declining in cities such as Seattle and Portland. Traffic was still heavy but now spread out over much longer periods, starting at 5 am and lasting until noon. Bizarre new patterns were cropping up, such as the "reverse commute" in Seattle as lots of male computer scientists at Microsoft, where I worked for nine years, in the suburb of Redmond, where I lived, raced downtown to find females—a weekday ritual called "the running of the programmers".

The current data are telling something else again. The baby-boomers are starting to retire, forcing employers to compete for new talent by letting younger employees work wherever they please. Even the older workers are becoming nomadic (I work around the world from my BlackBerry and laptop). Traffic congestion, though still bad, is for the first time not getting worse. Car-pooling, which "green" city governments are still encouraging, is declining sharply as commuting times and directions are becoming more diverse and more complex.

Indeed, even though there are as many cars on the roads as ever, they are now making very different journeys. In the previous decade trips followed a radial pattern, as both office workers and telecommuters ran errands away from their workplace and back again in order to check their voice messages and faxes. Now people are making trips in a daisy-chain pattern, more like how things have always been in Morocco. Nomads set off in the morning to drop off the kids at school and then spend the day hopping from one third place to another, with stops at the gym, the post office and so on. Throughout the day they remain connected to colleagues and family members who are elsewhere, and increasingly their movements form no discernible collective pattern at all. Just like the days inside the Kasbahs.

10. THE THINGS WE LEFT BEHIND

"They are closer to nature in a thousand ways: in their clothes, in the form of their shoes. Hence beauty is linked to everything they do. In our corsets, our tight shoes, our ridiculous sheaths, we inspire pity…Is this the price one pays for civilization and the bliss of having a round hat instead of a burnoose?"

—Eugène Delacroix, in a letter to his friend
Monsieur J.B. Pierret, 1848

This has whet an appetite for Kasbahs, so we drive 19 miles out of town to the Aït Benhaddou Kasbah, an architectural wonder that looks like a giant melting wedding cake on top of a tableland above the trickling Ouarzazate River. It looks terribly familiar, but perhaps because it has been featured in a number of Hollywood films, from *Lawrence of Arabia* to *Jewel of the Nile* to *Gladiator*. Ouarzazate has become such a haven for Hollywood desert films that it is often called Ouarzawood, and now an estimated 50,000 residents make their livings here in the film industry. Clochards and camels mill about outside by flowering almond trees, and blue-turbaned merchants wave us into their dark and cool shops for some tea. One woman holds out a small woven tray as I pass by, and thinking she is asking for alms for the poor I reach into my pocket for some dirhams…but as I look closer I see she is rather offering almonds for the rich, and so I buy a handful.

We locate a local guide—not a daunting task, as they lurk here in large knots, eager to pounce on any passing *Nasranis* ('foreigner,' or more exactly, 'Nazarenes,' 'Christians.') It would be a challenge of a different order if we sought a female guide, as this is a gender-specific business. Issmail Hossni won this lottery, as he is the coolest looking guide…he wears a hat of straw just dipped into the river. "Berber air conditioning," he calls it. He also wears an authentic-looking sports jersey, except that the home team is spelled "New Yorke."

Issmail leads us inside. It's a huge, unsettling labyrinthine place, that once raged with the lives of 500 people; now just forty-five families (including one Jewish) reside here, who help keep the proud customs and codes vibrant and continuous.

A solar panel spreads over the roof of one den, and I peer inside to see that it powers a small television. We work our way upwards, as though navigating a giant honeycomb. Low dim chambers open to vaulted chambers; winding passageways with stone staircases lead from floor to adobe floor; lintels dyed with indigo, henna and saffron patterns hold up ceilings of mud and palm fronds reinforced by palm crossbeams; between courtyards run dark tunnels; there are corbelled arches and machicolations of palm wood; there are secret rooms, granaries and wells. It is hot outside, but cool and confounding inside this Kasbah.

Up a long set of stairs, rounded by generations of fervent feet, we emerge at the uppermost level, and see that on an knoll further up there is a watchtower, crumbled and worn, as if flattened by the ferocity of the sun. Issmail has no interest in going further, so of course up I scramble solo to this eminence in the bullying light.

At the top I duck into a shadow behind a wall and open my arms wide to catch the trace of a delicate breeze. There is a powdery odor from the hot clay walls. The sun has beaten my hair into a liquid cap that drips down my temples. I pause for a sip from my water bottle, and then peer through a portal in the wall. Like shards of once-sharp glass smoothed by decades on a seabed, the walls of this watchtower are rounded, and the windows partially dissolved. But the Kasbah's strategic location is still quite evident, as it overlooks all the land, providing security as well as views. Kasbahs such as this were safe havens for families, for travelers and traders, and guards kept lookout for invaders from high fortified watchtowers. These well-protected edifices were one of the reasons Morocco was the only Arab country never to have been conquered by the Ottomans.

This Kasbah was a major stop on the north-south trade route. For centuries, caravans carried gold, silver, salt and slaves through here, and often stayed in this Kasbah. The passing nomads were in a way like bees pollinating flowers in gardens far from where they started, spreading knowledge, arts and cultures over a vast region. They brought different music, dance, foods, customs, crafts, beliefs, politics and new human constructs....the travelers and adventures found shelter and social interaction behind secure Kasbah walls, and seeds of multiculturalism were sown.

It's hot up here, watching for invaders....so on the way down I duck into one of the cool, dark warrens, and when my eyes acclimatize I find it is a shop dripping with yards of brightly colored yarn....the colors pop as though someone had burst a giant bag of Skittles. It is, of course, a rug shop, and by sitting down to cool on a nest of embroidery for a few seconds I am suddenly a target. Tea is poured, boiling hot and thick with sugar; sugar cookies are served; and several folks show up to unfurl the rugs. I stroke my palm over the knots of several tempting weaves, but somehow successfully resist....just the thought of carrying a rug down the mountain is enough to dissuade his persuasive presentation. But I offer a generous tip for the respite, and head on down. Looking back as we head to the hotel I watch as the soft rays of the setting sun gild the Kasbah.

I dine that night at La Maison Arabe with Laura Hubber of the BBC, who is doing a story on Ouarzawood for the World Service. She's just returned from taping at Atlas Studios, where she interviewed a guide/translator, Aimad, who's been at the studio for 26 years, since it started.

In the flickering light of cut-metal lamps—it looks like movie light—Laura tells me she saw quite an array of props, from the airplane used in *Jewel of the Nile*, to Cleopatra's barge, to a Roman Forum, to a Tibet house and Styrofoam stupas from *Kundun* (Scorsese brought in 350 Tibetans for nine months for the film); to a fake library and lots of fake gold. Whole cities have been constructed, from Jerusalem (for *Kingdom of Heaven* and *Passion of the Christ*) to Luxor. They just wrapped *Body of Lies*, with Leonardo diCaprio and Russell Crowe, and begin shooting an IMAX film on the great explorer Ibn Battuta tomorrow. "Hollywood loves Ouarzawood," she says. "Literally. Aimad says one of the key actors in *Kundun* married a Moroccan and never went home."

11. A WISE MAN KNOWS HE IS A FOOL

"The most beautiful of lands, paradise as far as the eyes can see.
Her earth is generous and hospitable. Her features speak her beauty…
The pride, charm and benevolence of her people are widely known.
So many have been captivated by my land.
Whoever asks should come and see for themselves.
Oh delight of my eye; the sun illuminates her
Bride between two shores; even the mountains sing for her.
Whoever is running from pain can visit our land and be healed.
Her natural environment is a medicine.
Whoever drinks her water recovers.
Our land is a place of solace.
A refreshing drink from a pure spring."
–Nouaman Lahlou, *Jebel Atlas*, 2003

The next day Fatima bides us goodbye as she needs to prepare for her wedding. "As-salam alaykum!" (May peace be upon you) she shouts as Mohammed starts the engine, and we wave goodbyes. The car turns east towards Merzouga. It's a desolate passage. The only things that grow here are Kasbahs, it seems. We pass Kasbah after Kasbah, many now converted to small hotels and coffee shops, their flat roofs sprinkled with corn cobs. We wind through the Draâ Valley, where at least one ancient explorer said was then inhabited by what he called "inhospitable Ethiopians living on land full of ferocious beasts." (The 'beasts' were probably croco-diles, the last Saharan specimen of which a French colonialist proudly exterminated in 1929.) Ethiopians, many believe, were the antecedents to the Berbers, and they wandered here from the Horn of Africa, as had I.

We detour from the main highway and switchback first up the Dades Gorge, with its deep, rocky grooves, herds of black goats, and small hanging villages that look as though with one good rainfall they would melt, like sugar cubes, completely into the ground. Then, beyond the village of Tinehir, we crash into the hem of the untamed world at the Todra Gorge, with its 1,000-foot-high sheer walls rising empty around us, and at our feet a taper that pinches the walls to within 30 feet of each other at one point. A sliver of sky separates the cliff faces at the top.

These walls have become a mecca for rock climbers in recent years, but there are none today. I hike up the gorge a ways, by spouts of sacred datura flowers, the trumpet of the devil for its hallucinogenic properties (when I was a guide on the Colorado River through the Grand Canyon I witnessed a woman who ate some datura seeds and disappeared into an alternative reality. On the second day we had her helicoptered out to the nearest hospital on the rim).

I amble past makeshift stalls selling turquoise necklaces and mirrors, to where the gorge opens up to direct sunlight and loses some of its sympathetic magic, and then turn around and relish in the shade of the narrowest spot. I cross a plank, wobbly as a leaf, over a sprite of a river, its clear, rushing waters filled with fish, and am tempted to splash in. Morocco is blessed with eternal springs…clean, fresh water that spills from all sides of the four major mountain ranges (70% of the country is mountainous). Water is the natural nexus for all living things, trees, animals and people who travel. It is one of the reasons Morocco evolved as the tolerant crossroads of Africa. Even its brand of Islam is tolerant, though it has rejected the more radical tenets of a sect that first troubled Moroccans in 1811. Then, King Saud of the Arabian Peninsula called upon leaders around the Arab world to adopt Wahhabism, the austere brand of Islam gaining adherents among Bedouin tribes. The precursor of modern-day Islamic fundamentalism, Wahhabism held that the Koran must be understood as the literal truth. Wahhabism came to dominate Saudi Arabia, but it did not take hold in Morocco. Today Morocco has the cleanest human rights record in Africa and the Middle East, and promotes a broadmindedness that is not so common in much of the world.

All of this means Morocco has *baraka*. It's a notion found in Morocco, and in Swahili-speaking East Africa, that a person, creature or place is blessed. The blessing runs so deeply that it touches every cell, every atom, and anyone who comes in contact with the baraka is also then so blessed. Witness the rise of our aptly named president.

Mohammed parks the car in the shade of a cliff, and we step across a plank for sandwiches and tea at the Hotel Jasmina, which hangs just above the river in the heart of the Todra Gorge. It's a jovial place, wide open on a narrow bench in the canyon. I watch our tea-maker after our order. He takes a long-handled tin canister and puts in heaping teaspoons of green China tea (the label says Formosan chun mee). Next he adds five teaspoons of sugar. Another little canister filled with hot water from the samovar is already embedded in a spread of coals. When it boils, he pours the water over the mixed tea and sugar. While it is steeping he crushes as many stalks of fresh spearmint as he can into a glass. Then he strains the tea into the glass, garnishing it with a sprig of verbena and three unopened orange blossoms. The result is hot, sweet, strongly aromatic, bearing very little resemblance to any tea in America. It is, our waiter says, *até,* a refresher in its own right.

As we sip our minty tea the man adjacent, a stranger, dabs his lips with a napkin, articulates his body towards us, offers his hand, and makes an introduction. He is Nouaman Lahlou, one of the most popular singers in Morocco. Born in Fès, Nouaman studied the famed Egyptian Oud master "Mohammed Abdel-Wahad. " Now he has found his own renown for mixing elements of his eastern classical oud training with modern composition, and for blending Egyptian pop rhythms with old Moroccan melodies and lyrics. He hands me one of this CDs, and tells me, "Music is the key to understanding Morocco," and then he turns to sign an autograph for some of his fans who just discovered his presence in the little tea room.

There are Berbers and Arabs sitting side-by-side in this café, a not uncommon sight throughout the kingdom. But despite the egalitarian tenets of Islam, this river valley once flowed with blood.

When the Arabs invaded in the 7th century the Berbers embraced Islam, but as a result of exploitative Arab taxes, discrimination and slaving raids, they soon raised revolts in the name of their new religion's egalitarian ideals. In the 11th century the nomadic Berbers overthrew the Arabs and established the pious Almoravid state, the first of three Berber dynasties to rule Morocco. The Berber dynasties, dominated by tribal warlords, could not unite the country or control its rural regions. In the 15th century the Portuguese took advantage of Morocco's disunity and began occupying cities along the Atlantic and Mediterranean coasts. Soon they tried to penetrate the interior. It was left to the Arabs of this region to unite Moroccans under the banner of Islam and expel the infidels. Yet it was the Arabs who presided over the colonization of the country under the French, and then emerged as Morocco's rulers when independence came in 1956.

Despite this violent past I am threatened only with a surfeit of tea and hospitality.

12. FIELD OF DUNES

"This sand seemed to us the connecting link between land and water. It was a kind of water on which you could walk, and you could see the ripple-marks on its surface, produced by the winds, precisely like those at the bottom of a brook or lake. We had read that Mussulmans are permitted by the Koran to perform their ablutions in sand when they cannot get water, a necessary indulgence in Arabia, and we now understand the propriety of this provision."
–Henry David Thoreau, 1849

We pass through the market town of Erfoud, and through a moonscape of black shale to arrive near sunset at Merzouga, an oasis at the edge of the Erg Chebbi Dunes, less than 25 miles far from the Algerian border, where these ergs originated. An "erg" is a slow moving sand dune, kind of like an ocean wave moving in eon time, and across which the "ships of the desert," the wide-hoofed camels, sail.

We drive through an arch into what is labeled "Tourist Village," and indeed it has traditional tourist architecture, including an oversized papier-mâché camel. The high walls are capped with upwards stabbing shards of broken bottles so the tourists won't escape.

Legend has it that the dunes of Erg Chebbi were created by God as punishment to the locals who refused shelter to a passing woman and her child. He sent the sandstorm that buried the village, and the lesson learned lives today in the culture of hospitality that imbues the Sahara. There is here a root belief in selflessness. In Morocco to be selfless one gives charity anonymously, walks softly on the earth, and looks out for others—even total strangers who knock at the Kasbah door. For the Moroccan mind the self is an obstacle, an impediment, in humanity's quest for real progress.

We park in front of a newly-built, square-towered Kasbah made of the ubiquitous mud-straw *pisé*, the Kanz Erremal – "desert treasure" in Berber—and slope through the cool atrium, past the swimming pool, directly onto the sands of the Sahara.

Stepping over a large black scarab beetle, I meet our cameleer, Ahmed Fayou, a man who seems to keep the heat of the desert away with his natural coolness. He instructs my one-humped Arabian camel to kneel, its front legs doubling over until they touch the ground. I throw one leg over the folded blankets on his arched back, and grab the pommel with both hands. My camel roars, then does his boat-rock rise, and I look down at his feet. They are big, round, splayed and padded, swollen looking, soft and squishy, like giant cat paws without the nails.

Ahmed takes off his rubber-tire sandals, and with a nylon tether in one hand that connects to a carabineer in the camel's left nostril, he leads the caravan into the sand. The ruffles and flutes of sand run in a line, almost perfectly in a north-south direction, and mark the western fringe of the Sahara Desert, dividing Morocco from Algeria.

This is Chakib's first camel ride, and he has donned a jungle camel-flage shirt, a pair of shorts (unusual attire for most

Moroccans), and a pair of flip-flops for the ride. His Tag Heuer catches sparks of light from the lowering sun as his camel lashes him back and forth in a movement a bit like Latin dancing.

The camels gait along with no hint of hurry, even though this is rush hour in the Sahara. Back home, in Los Angeles, at this hour I am often stuck in traffic, choked not merely with pollution, but with the emissions of haste, rage and cell towers. Here there is none of that nonsense.

At one point my camel curves her long neck back on itself and we exchange glances; she almost seems to be flirting with her glistening bulb-eyes…I can't help but notice she seems to have large French eyelashes…quite seductive…. but British teeth. There is an undeniable beauty, though, in her mucus-sodden eyes and pouting blubbery lips. It is perhaps not a coincidence that the Arabic word for beauty, *jamal,* is the same for camel. To the nomads of Morocco camels are the belles of the desert, inspiring whispered compliments and poetic accolades. Yet they are more than just pretty faces. In liberating the denizens of the Sahara from life in oasis towns and making navigational the great sand seas surrounding them, camels are nothing less than the progenitors of nomad identity.

Native to the Arabian Peninsula and introduced into Morocco with the Arab invasion that brought Islam, the single-humped *Camelus dromedaries,* can, in one session at the well, drink more than twenty gallons. It can go without drinking for five days in summer and two weeks in winter; man can go but one. The camel masters however, if in a dry pickle, can shove a stick down their charge's throat and drink the vomited water. Using a sharpened straw they can sip blood from its jugular; they can wash their hair in its urine. Camels also provide milk, meat, fur, medicine and hide for tents; the combustible nuggets of their bouncy dung serve as fuel and fertilizer (Morocco is the world's largest exporter of what is referred to as "crude fertilizer"). The Arabic language contains over 1000 words to describe camels and their various breeds and states of maturity. The Bedouin call the desert *sahel*, "ocean," and camels are the ships of this desert.

As we ride a landscape more sky than earth, the light changes the sand from beige to pumpkin to scarlet, and the shadows form ever shifting patterns and textures, akin to abstract art. Ergs are migratory, like the nomads they host. These are crescent-shaped with gentle windward slopes, up which the grains slowly creep and settle. They have steep leeward faces, down which sand avalanches sometimes cascade. The dunes multiply in ever more dense colonies, and eventually they link to form sculptured chains perpendicular to the prevailing winds. Some are quite high, over 600' from tip to trough, among the highest in the Sahara.

Though hired by the Middle East Anti-Locust Unit to search out locust breeding grounds, Wilfred Thesiger, who was born in Ethiopia, pursued a personal quest across the desert, a quest intimately related to the nomads with whom he lived: he hoped to "find peace that comes from solitude, and among the Bedouin, comradeship in a hostile world." The spirit of the Bedouin, he wrote, "lit the desert like a flame." He at first felt like "an uncouth and inarticulate barbarian, an intruder from a shoddy and materialistic world." After five years in the desert Thesiger emerged hardened by heat and thirst, and for the rest of his life (he died in 2003) he felt himself a stranger in 'civilized' company. He had found what he was looking for in the desert, and it had transformed him.

We ride until dark, and then dismount at a crest and walk the final few hundred yards down a steep dune. Our footfalls send cascades of sand down steep sides with the fluidity of water. At first it seems we are pitching into darkness; then around one dune there is a point of light….a lantern, and we make our way to a makeshift camp of Berber tents. We drop anchor, and I pull out my canteen and offer Ahmed a drink, but he is bent down tying our camels for the night and shakes his head no. "Always trust in Allah," he winks, "but tie your camel first."

Dinner is chick eas, a thick soup called *harira,* and goat meat kabobs; the fire flickers goblins against the sand, but wait…one is real…a three-toed skink darts across the sand. I snatch the lizard as it approaches my lap, and stare into its wide eyes. It twitches its head, darts a blue tongue, and stares back, its unflinching gaze and ancient wrinkles making it seem immeasurably wise. I set it back on the sand, where it stands accusingly for a beat, and then scurries off into the darkness.

The guides play goat-skin drums and hand cymbals as after-dinner entertainment, and then I retire to an outdoor cot and tuck myself in under thick camelhair blankets. Chakib, who has never camped before, blows gently into his fists and tells me he is going to sleep within the folds of one of the sheep wool tents.

I watch the shooting stars for a spell, then fall into the old daily habit at home: I check my BlackBerry. Thankfully, there is no service here. Just before I left the travel site TripAdvisor (which is owned by Expedia, a company at which I was among the founding executives) polled 3000 travelers asking about their travel habits and trends. Twenty-eight percent of the respondents said they check email at least daily when on a long weekend vacation, up from 22 percent the previous year. When on a vacation of a week or more, 39 percent said they check email at least once a day, compared to 30 percent last year. What does that mean? For me, it suddenly puts value on this place with no connectivity except with the earth and the sky. The desert's most precious gift may be to teach us to be alone with ourselves.

We are in a quiet place with no water, and the question churns, why come here? The Sahara is the largest and most austere place on Earth. The Great Nothing, the Endless Emptiness. It's a place of sand-blasted stones on desert floor, a wilderness of sand and barren rock. The Fearful Void. Why come here?

The answer, said Paul Bowles, in a letter published shortly before his death in 1999, is that when a person has been here, "and undergone the baptism of solitude, he can't help himself. Once he has been under the spell of the vast, luminous, silent country, no other place is quite strong enough for him, no other surroundings can provide the supremely satisfying sensation of existing in the midst of something that is absolute. He will go back, whatever the cost in comfort or money, for the absolute has no price."

T.E. Lawrence, no stranger to the strange land of the desert, found himself captivated by its allure, and seduced by its incantatory charms.

"By the day the hot sun fermented us; and we were dizzied by the beating wind," the British military intelligence officer wrote in *Seven Pillars of Wisdom*, in 1922.

"At night we were stained by dew, and shamed into pettiness by the innumerable silences of the stars."

As my eyelids slump the stars seem to pull me up into the soft center of their lights, and the earth beneath me shrinks to the size of my body. Silence is a thought I can't empty from my head. It invades me, pushes against my inner skin. A camel roar makes the silence take flight for a second, but it lands again. The clamor of quiet finally pushes me to sleep.

In the middle of the night I awake to the slight sound of someone's foot landing on the sand, the grains compressing and shifting. At first I think it is a thief, and flop over, like an egg in a pan, to inspect the source while reaching for my BlackBerry with one hand, thinking it the only weapon at my disposal. But I can make out the silhouette, and recognize it as Chakib, who is, I now hear, just out of his tent to undrink the day.

With the dawn I awake to dunes so lusciously golden and honeyed I'm tempted to lick them. The camels, swishing their tails, flicking their heavy-lashed eyes, are being unhobbled. *"Utsh! Utsh!"* Ahmed coaxes his charges. We pack up, and begin the slow ride back to captivity. It is quiet and cool in the morning air, yet nobody can hear me whisper to my camel—or his whispering back to me. My tracks disappear behind me, covered by a soft wind. Wind is good for the Sahara; it makes everything new.

Here lies solitude of a kind, far removed from cell phones, iPods and BlackBerries, away from the madding swarms of the big city—a place, de Villiers and Hirtle wrote in *Sahara, The Extraordinary History of the World's Largest Desert*, "as remote and perilous as it is possible to be," where some come to seek solace.

"Hoping to find their center by becoming lost in the eternal; hoping, perhaps, that the soul can be healed there."

As my camel pauses for a call, Ahmed stoops and picks up a fist of sand, and lets it drain through his fingers. He looks at this moment like a figure from a 19th-century Arabian daguerreotype. He tells me that a new type of traveler has been showing up here of late: solace and healing-seeking tourists who come mid-summer, when it is often over 120 degrees, who then ask to be buried in the sand and baked in belief the technique will cure rheumatism.

My camel seems to be coaxing the dunes, as little swirls of sand follow her footsteps. "Richard, Richard," the wind seems to whisper. A travelogue makes for haphazard argument, but the Koran speaks in promise. In this place where sand and sun have weight; a world of want and rare rains and certain death, it is easy to appreciate the appeal of the Koran's description of the afterlife. It promises ascension to "lofty chambers of Paradise underneath which rivers flow," to "Gardens of Bliss" where the faithful recline on sofas, "a cup from a spring being passed round to them, white, a delight to the drinkers, wherein no sickness is, neither intoxication, and with them wide-eyed maidens restraining their glances as if they were hidden pearls." They would find themselves "robed in silk and brocade," enjoying "fruits and palm trees and pomegranates," sampling "rivers of water unstalling, rivers, too, of milk unchanging in flavor…" gazing upon "*houris* (virgins) cloistered in cool pavilions."

A place of unsettling beauty, and of great privation, this is. A cathedral of sand—part refuge, part sanctuary and, for some, a deep grave. Ahmed describes the bleak script of this place, such as the tale of a Czech woman who wandered in here, and was found dead from heat exhaustion the next day. And of several folks who died in a freak flashflood in May of 2006. The lesson of the Sahara: there is still a very big place in the world where people, without their gadgets and amour, are fragile animals indeed.

The American guide and old friend Kristy Larson told me a tale about one of her camel safaris in the desert here. It was late December 2007 and she and her clients were driving eastward from Zagora into the Sahara. They had been driving all day on 4-wheel drive tracks; sometimes on no tracks at all. About 4 pm they were crossing the Mud River, or Oued Rheris, where they had to make their own tracks. The Mud River is only full of mud when it rains heavily in the High Atlas and then the water flashes south into the Sahara. This trip the river was dry, but still it was a difficult trek through dunes, bushes and dried muddy areas. Sometimes it took an hour to cross one stretch of the river bed. They had just finished one such crossing when they saw three large bright blue packages—perhaps 18 inches by 18 inches—

scattered in the middle of nowhere on the eastern edge of the Mud River.

Just a mile south was Algeria; they weren't far from the small village of Rhemila. Kristy told her driver, Ayed, to stop. So they stopped and picked up the packages. They were very heavy—maybe 30 or 40 lbs., and covered with bright blue woven plastic, which was very strong—Kristy used this same plastic to weave around her air freight shipments of handicrafts from Morocco. Kristy then shouted, "Ahh, maybe they are books!! So, she opened a couple of the packages and found not books but rather tightly wrapped bricks of hashish. She couldn't believe her eyes. She suddenly looked around, and wondered if they were being watched; perhaps this was a drop-off point, or a smuggling route from Algeria. So, she left the packages in the desert, and hid the bricks she had opened behind a bush and hastened on to her campsite in the dunes—hoping no one had seen her, and wondering the truth behind the incident. The desert holds so many secrets.

Before leaving I decide to indulge in a new trend…I rent a pair of well-used Rossignal skis from a local shop (which also sells tribal rugs), and trek to the top of a sand dune, and point down slope. I was told some skiers get up to 30 miles an hour schussing these slopes, but I barely move. It's more like skiing sandpaper than powder. It's too late in the day, Ahmed says, even though it is still shy of 8:00 am…the sand is already too dry. Come back again, he invokes, and I am tempted.

13. WIZARDS OF 212

"Faith is to believe what you do not see; the reward of this faith is to see what you believe."
–St. Augustine of Hippo, 410 AD

The next morning, in the first blush of pink light, we head north. We carve our way up through the Middle Atlas, alongside a watercourse lined with dwarf palms. Not an hour after we begin we approach what appears to be a group of very short people toiling by the side of the road. The 19th-century scholar R. G. Haliburton had written a monograph entitled *The Dwarfs of the Atlas Mountains,* in which he claimed that for 3000 years the Moors had succeeded in making a secret of the existence of a race of dwarfs here, until, that is, they revealed all to him in 1890. Mr. Haliburton's explanation was that the dwarfs were regarded by the Moors as holy men. One Moor said to Mr. Haliburton, "It is a sin to speak about them to you. I shall say nothing." Another said, "God has sent them to us. We must not talk about them." They were believed to bring good luck, and act as guardians and protectors, like the Palladium of the Trojans.

Of course it was with great anticipation and excitement that I ask Mohammed to slow down so we can get a good look at this lost race (there has been no record of the secret dwarfs since Haliburton), but as we glide closer the short folks turn towards our vehicle and I see they are children…pre-teens out on some field day collecting flowers by the road.

We continue to zigzag north, on a road with more corrections than the Dow. We're heading towards Ifrane, a town justly juxtaposed to any in the Sahara. The first hour we drive through a wild landscape that looks like the surface of a forgotten planet; sand sprays across the road in lacy sheets. I imagine with enough wind one could drown in the desert here. Near a bump in the road called Akhbou Oujaabou we stop at a natural geyser that sprouts from the friable earth, at a point where natural fossils, some millions of years old, such as ammonites, trilobites, and orthomerus have been unearthed, remnants from the ocean that lapped here some 350 million years ago. I resist the merchants selling these minerals and stones as I can't tell zirconium from zinc.

We coil up the road above the spritely turquoise Oued Ziz, through the long fertile limestone-encased Ziz Valley. This is a valley of illusions. Villages appear that seem to be frozen in mid-tumble down the surrounding mountains. At one point I stare at a mirage of water in the desert, and even mention the optical illusion to Mohammed, who smiles archly and calls it an *aghmam*….the mirage doesn't evaporate….it's real, the vast emerald lake behind the Hassan Addakhil Dam. At another point I watch as a bush starts to trot down the shore at the village of Ait Othman, but then reveals itself as a donkey carrying a load of firewood. "That's the Berber 4-wheel drive," Chakib quips.

As with the women who have been key to keeping the argan tree and its by-products alive and vital, the women in the Ziz Valley are known as keepers of the fig. They pass along traditional knowledge about how best to irrigate the fields, how to select the best seeds for planting, and what times are best to plant and harvest for greatest yields. These women have kept this valley a leader in fig production, and in its palm-lined beauty.

At the northern end of the road is the Tunnel de Légionnaire, built by French colonial troops in the 1930s, in order to create a passageway from the mountains to the Ziz valley. Just beyond the tunnel, up from the road, is the font of the Ziz, the Source Bleue de Meski, a natural spring that has a reputation for inspiring fertility. Young women bathe by candlelight in the waters of the source grotto, and emerge as fruitful as the surrounding apricot trees.

For lunch we stop at the French garrison town of Midelt at the base of Jbel Ayachi, a 12,264' peak that looks from here like a bubble in a blue cauldron. The town is festooned with banners, ribbons and fluttering red Moroccan flags, as King Mohammed VI, the direct descendent of the prophet, and 23rd in line in the Alaouite Dynasty, had visited a few hours before us, and performed the Friday prayers at the Sidi Mohamed Belarbi El Alaoui Mosque. We pause for a light lunch of fresh tomatoes and cheese at the Restaurant Le Pin, and then head down the road less than a mile to the Kasbah Myriem & Monastere Notre-dame de L'Atlas, which features a workshop run by Franciscan sisters who teach Berber women weaving and embroidery. There are five Franciscan monks living in the monastery, while six nuns live in a house right across the street, and a dozen Berber women are busy weaving on the black and white tiled floor set into Escher-like patterns, while four more are working the woolen wefts as though plucking harps playing *Flight of the Bumblebee*. Because the carpets are made without patterns, no two are alike.

It seems odd to see Caucasian Franciscans in the heart of Morocco teaching Berber women a trade, but then maybe not....it's all part of the fabric here. And it is, I assume, one of the few shops where one can buy a carpet at a fair price and not haggle, so I pick a patterned throw rug and purchase it from an elderly French sister, Nicole Debono, for the tagged price. It isn't until I am home that I compare the experience with my friend Patty Conroy, who bought a similar carpet from the same coop; Patty tells me that she bargained with the nuns and picked up her rug for half of what I paid.

We wind upwards through forests of cedars, to the mile-high village of Ifrane, and suddenly it seems we've fallen through a wormhole and emerged in alpine France. The first sign we pass as we enter the village is for the Hotel Le Chamonix, and everything beyond is themed as though in the Alps. The houses, some Tudor-timbered, many painted white, are steeply eaved and covered with those quintessentially European rolled red tiles. Gardens are bedecked with flowering shrubs and ornamental trees reminiscent of Provence.

Ifrane was constructed by the French colonial administration in the late 1920s, and as it is nestled in pines and snow-bound for much of the year, the home-sick designers tried to replicate a resort in the Alps. This is the first time on this trip I've donned layers, including an Ex Officio vest. It's chilly. No wonder. Ifrane recorded the lowest temperature ever recorded in Africa, minus 23 degrees Celsius.

Chakib folds his arms against the cold and says he's going to motor onwards. He'll catch up with me again in Rabat, where it's warmer, he says.

14. MEET ME AT THE KASBAH

"Man is born free, and everywhere he is in chains."
—Jean-Jacques Rousseau, 1762

From Ifrane we downshift down the hill, another hour north, through a jeweled blur of waving red poppies, to the imperial city of Fès, where I had once found myself lost in the medina. At one of the first traffic circles entering the city there is a fountain with a globe of the world that floats and spins at the apex, a fitting totem perhaps for the convulsions of the world, and a place that so seethes with humanity. Over half a million people, some guess (it would be impossible to know with any certainty), live within the medina walls, and perhaps as many cats. Walter Harris, who as the *London Times* man in Morocco at the start of the 20th-century enjoyed the friendship of the sultans, said Fès smelled of incense and dead cats.

We stop in at the Palais M' Nebhi, where France and Morocco signed the protectorate treaty in 1912. Beneath its extravagantly painted wood muqaranas, and upon its polished Moorish tiles, we have couscous and tea, and then climb to its rooftop for a panorama of the city. There, as though a diorama writ large, is the Oued el-Jawahir, the River of Pearls, on whose banks the city was founded. There are ancient sun-burned walls, rectangular mosques scratching the sky, cemeteries with oblong graves in white (white is the color of mourning in Islam), and the sea of white satellite dishes glittering on coppery roofs. I'm tempted to once again dive in, so I step down the stairs, and back into the eventful streets. But as I enter the great gate known as the Bab Bou Jeloud, as I did a few years back, into the shadowed passages of the medina, it feels like falling through layers of history and ending up just short of the present.

I am once again assaulted by familiar aromas that define invisible boundaries: coffee, cloves, olive oil, rose water, urine, mint, the sweet scent of cedar shavings, the tang of onions frying, the acrid smoke of burning charcoal. Sounds waft, too, like smoke: childish choruses of recitation from behind the shutters of tiny Koranic schools; the rhythmic clang of coppersmiths; the klaxon shouts of porters bent double under piles of sheep skins or tottering towers of shoe boxes. Add the mantric cries of beggars, the bells of water vendors, the layered strains of muezzins calling the faithful to prayer, never quite in unison, from every minaret in the city as the sun slides off the rooftops. It is all the same, yet fresh. In the Sufi school of Muslim theology, the enlightened soul is said to comprehend that, just as permanence is contained within flux, so change is contained within repetition. The world is in intense motion, ascending to meet the descent of the Absolute in manifested forms. The flow occurs in such an orderly, successive manner, according to definite patterns, that we are unaware of it. Here in the medina of Fès the only suppression is the passage of time. It is, I am convinced, a kind of "fezzy logic."

It's time for a drink at the L'Alcazar Bar in the Riad Fès. I need something to spike the thin milk of my musings. I sit in front of a bowl of salted groundnuts still in their dark wine skins and order a cold beer. On the next stool over sits slumped a Frenchman. He nurses his brew, and then strikes up a conversation…strangers do talk in bars here. After the small talk he tells me he was in town shopping for his own riad, a popular real estate purchase in recent years. But he has given up. It's all too confusing here, he says. He shares a popular story about a Frenchman who had bought a sprawling medieval palace and then went out to buy some milk for his tea. He hurried home with the milk, but was never able to find the house again.

After the pilsner I step outside, and as I gaze about the medina this time I notice something. Or rather I don't see something….In the midst of all the bustle I don't see a single person with a cell phone, PDA or any digital device. Rather, folks are mingling, interacting, buying, selling, negotiating, gossiping, and otherwise delighting in one another's company. Everything is brazenly public here. Strangers and family and old friends are in a never-ending discourse, spirited and passionate, full of touch and eye contact and smile and the exchange of goods and ideas. And they take their time.

Time is timeless here, endless and circular, as in the endless arabesques. Time is something people seem to have plenty of here. While westerners get annoyed with small inconveniences and delays, Moroccans have a saying: "He who hurries has one foot in the grave."

What would Rousseau have made of the modern-day balls and chains with which we westerners now shackle ourselves? They are not made of steel or iron, but of silicon and plastic and digits and electrons and waves zooming through the air. These are the chains of all kinds of devices: the BlackBerry, the iPhone , the Android, the Slash, the Instinct, even the Walkman. These are the chains with which we have bound ourselves, losing much of our solitude and our ability to see the world around and inside us.

Consider a coffee shop in any city in America. We listen to music. We read books and newspapers. We email; we browse the web; we work on the laptop....but we don't talk to strangers. It's as though we've been injected with some sort of emotional Botox, suppressing the ability to express genuine feelings in public.

The bonds of obligation, like handcuffs, are clapped back onto our wrists, and we shuffle through the day in servitude to our jobs and our mundane tasks. We're part of an immense, all-engulfing machine of communication and control. Human flesh and spirit become plastic and electronic machinery.

What if we didn't have cell phones or P.D.A.'s, as most Moroccans? We would still have duties and families and bosses, but they would not be at our heels, yipping at us constantly, barking at us to do this or that or worry about this or that. We would have some moat of time and space around ourselves. Not now.

Consider another example: Walk down any downtown street in America. Almost every man and woman is on the phone or scanning the screen of a device or thumbing a BlackBerry. No one looks at anyone else. It is as if each person were in a cocoon of electrons and self-obsession and obligation. Each of these people might as well be wearing a yoke around his neck.

There is no community within these walls—People are hermetically sealed off from one another, not taking in the air or the architecture or the blue bowl of sky or just the miracle of confronting the earth as it is.

Now, there is no thought or reverie. There is nothing but gossip and making plans to shop or watch television or YouTube. The cell phone and the digital devices have basically replaced thought. Many years ago when I was building the adventure travel company Sobek, I had an office with a large window that opened to John Yost's office, my partner. We shared every conversation, idea and meeting....we communed with one another .We had shared mental space. That is not the dynamic at Microsoft, or Expedia or Yahoo, all places where I have hung my hat.

But in Morocco people still have some freedom of thought. They walk along the streets without phones. They wander the souks and through Kasbahs without any talking over the airwaves. They talk to one another. They look up at the clear sky. There is a dance to their tread. Children line up to swing on a rope and then drop into the creek. Businesspeople walk to their appointments, greeting the people they see, not talking to a small plastic box. Moroccans are connected to the glorious sheltering sky and water and land, and, most of all, connected to their own ruminations.

What would we do if cell phones and the pings in our pockets disappeared? We would be forced to think again. We would have to confront reality. What I have seen of the loss of solitude and dignity is terrifying among those who travel and work, or even who stay still and work. They are slaves to connectedness. Their work has become their indentured servitude. Their children and families are bound to the same devices, too. If ever there was a candidate for strict Congressional oversight, it is these cunning little devices.

But try a day without that invasion of your privacy. Or a week. You will be shocked at what you discover. It's called life. It's called nature. It's called getting to know one's self. I was on a raft trip recently down the Green River in Utah. After the third day in the canyons of Ladore I found that without my phone, without my BlackBerry, I came to know the people who traveled with me. And time seeped like syrup.

15. REPLACEABLE UNTIL IT'S NOT

"I know that as I go deeper into the city it seizes me and makes me entity, quantum, brick among bricks, lizard, dust—without me needing to be aware of it. Is it not the city of the Lords?"
– Driss Chraidi, 1954

As I think about this my nose begins to twitch, and I realize I've stumbled into a new quarter: the tannery of Fès. One trade that has never hurried is tanning. I climb the stairs to a leather boutique that overlooks what appears to be a series of oversized inkwells…they are, in fact, the vats of the ancient tannery, largest in Africa, still very much employed by some 250 families. I watch as men with trousers rolled up, others in loincloths, crouch over vast stone vats filled with multicolored dyes, dipping animal hides and then working them by hand and feet, a method unchanged since the 11th century. The vats contain a combination of animal fat, pigeon droppings, chemicals and urine, used to cure the skins. The skins spend 35 days in the brew to soften and dye, and each day the leather must be turned by hand. The backbreaking work is well paid, compensation for coagulated smells that could fell a horse. "It is Chanel No. 6," says Mohammed Mohoub, a "leather guide" in the shop.

He dials back how his product finds its way to his loft. Before the skins are soaked in natural pigments—"red from poppies, blue from indigo, orange from henna, brown from cedar wood, yellow from saffron, green from mint"—they must first be placed in vats "filled with limestone, water and pigeon excrement."

This last substance, he says, is delivered daily from pigeon coops all over the medina. (Some of these pigeons do double duty, ending up as pastillas served in the restaurants here).

"It contains ammoniac," he explains. "It makes the leather soft," and he points to the slippers, shoes, hats, pouffes and bags that adorn his shop. He is such a happy soul with such a wacky sense of humor, that I can't resist, and offer to negotiate for a leather bag. He starts at 500 dirhams, and I counter with 400, and we laugh and poke fun at one another. Finally I agree to 460, and he touches his hand to his heart to seal the deal. I know he got the best of the matter, but the transaction was enjoyable, the journey better than the destination, which is never truer than in the medina of Fès.

Summoning the last of my eagerness. I ask Mohammed if he knows someone who knows all the medina who might be a guide this time around,. He replies glossily, "if someone says he knows all the medina, he is lying." And so I decide to surrender to the puzzle.

I take a more leisurely stroll this time, meandering like the countless stray cats, stopping to dance with a couple of whirring Gnawa musicians, to drink from a spigot that spills into a communal basin carved into a tiled wall, to watch the ballet of metal workers hammer their bowls, and turn sheets of metal into exquisite appliqué lamps . Everywhere the medina hisses and clanks with the creation of handmade products; everywhere is the smoke of twisted history. The henna souk once held the largest mental asylum in the Merenid Empire. It also functioned as a hospital for storks, up until the Second World War. The medina is no more open to working sense than the working out of pi.

"In Fès there is only one age and one style, that of yesterday," wrote the twin brothers Jérôme and Jean Tharaud in the 1930s, and the yesterdays have gotten stronger and longer since. I step into an old *caravanserai*, which was kind of like a motel for caravans, and there were once hundreds in Fès. The buildings were tall; the animals would eat and sleep on the ground floor while the merchants would take rooms upstairs. This caravanserai now houses three-generations of a family of weavers, who hand-craft *jalabas,* the popular ankle-length garments that slip over the head, covering the entire body, with a pointed hood that usually just hangs down the back, the same garb worn by the ewoks in Star Wars. Counterintuitively, perhaps, the hoods are worn up in the midday sun, as they prevent the sun from hitting the head and skin and evaporating perspiration, the body's coolant. It also creates a minor draught that rises between the fabric and the skin.

The garments are sewn from a combination of wool, vegetable silk and cotton. One weaver wearing a Dolce Gabbana T-shirt explains as he shoots his flying shuttle back and forth across the loom that it takes about six hours and 3,600 threads to make one three-by-two meter *jalaba*, with its own distinct pattern, a designer robe so to speak.

There are, some estimate, some 200 fountains, 200 bathhouses, 200 hundred Koranic schools and 300 mosques in

The author, photo by Walker Bangs

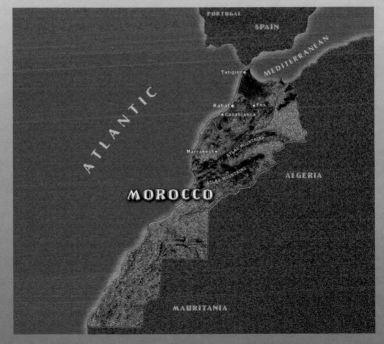

The author in front of Ait Ben Haddou, photo by Small World Productions

In the bazaar, photo by Walker Bangs

A caravan passing through the dunes of Erg Chebbi, photo by Beatrice Belguiral
(www.flickr.com/photos/color-de-la-vida)

The author hiking in the Atlas Mountains, photo by Small World Productions

Harvesting rose petals, photo by Small World Productions

A women's cooperative, photo by Small World Productions

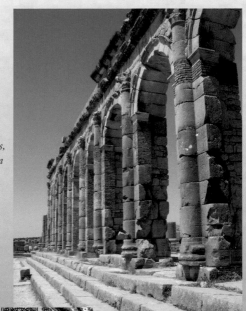

Roman ruins of Volubilis, photo by MsAnthea from flickr.com

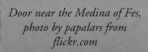

Door near the Medina of Fes, photo by papalars from flickr.com

The author skiing in the Sahara, photo by Small World Productions

Performers in native dress, photo by Small World Productions

Berber guide, photo by Small World Productions

Horsemen guard the Hassan mosque in Rabat, photo by Small World Productions

Hassan II Mosque in Casablanca, photo by papalars from flickr.com

the medina. I eddy out of the undulating currents to peek into the great Karaouiyine Mosque, said to be built in 857 AD. I watch as a man and his young son take off their shoes, cross the pillared courtyard, roll up their sleeves and proceed to drink and wash their hands, face and feet three times in the tiled fountain before heading to the interior to say their prayers, a hall off limits to non-Muslims, but one that supposedly can hold 20,000 worshipers. I feel like I am peeping onto some illicit scene, but can't pull my eyes away.

Fès doesn't proceed in a narrative order. Its glimpsed images are like scattered bones, disconnected from the skeleton of its ancient plot. For a thousand years or more it was the cultural center of Morocco, and, as such, was home to numerous *medersas,* or Islamic universities. "There is not a foot of ground in Fès where a wise man hasn't lived," goes an old saying, paying homage to the medersas. The Karaouiyine Mosque is touted as the oldest center of learning in the western world, pre-dating Oxford and the Sorbonne. Its library holds over 30,000 books, including a 9th century Koran. Many great thinkers and explorers studied here, including some of my superheroes: Ibn Battuta, who was born in Tangier in 1304 and set off after his studies to travel almost all the known world from Samarkand to Timbuktu; and the 16th century traveler Leo Africanus, who after being captured by European pirates and sold into slavery and then freed by Pope Leo X, put together the most comprehensive survey of Africa at that time for the Vatican.

Chakib and many in Morocco can quote easily and extensively from the Koran, which seems perhaps superfluous in a place known for its many libraries, and curious in the age of Google, when any passage can be found anytime, anywhere, on a number of different devices. But the power of memory is important in Morocco, and regarded as a blessed act in itself. According to Islamic tradition, the Angel Gabriel recited the Holy Book to the Prophet Mohammed over a period of about twenty years. Mohammed, who was illiterate, committed the entire text to memory as he received it, just as his disciples did, and many Moroccans continue to do today.

But at the battle of Yamahah, little more than a decade after Mohammed's flight from Mecca, so many of his followers were killed that there was a real fear the knowledge of the sacred text would be lost altogether. It was then that the Koran was written out for the first time.

Nearby is the Bou Inania, which has served as mosque, cathedral, students' residence and school for more than 600 years. Lost and distracted by the chaos of the streets, I passed this miracle of medieval Islamic architecture without noticing it on my last visit. Not this round.

In a single stride I pass from chaos to order, from the commercial hurly-burly of the lane to the calm repose of this extraordinary interior. Bou Inania is in retirement, its academic career over, which is why faithless characters such as me are allowed in. It is one of the finest buildings in Morocco and ranks among the best in the Islamic world.

The courtyard is a space of the most exquisite proportions. Its interior walls bear three bands of dense decoration rising from courtyard to the roof beams: zellige tiles, stucco work and cedar wood. The patterns—floral, geometric, calligraphic—are dizzyingly intricate. They enclose the courtyard with an elaboration of design that is almost beyond measure, certainly beyond my comprehension. The effect is not what I expect. Such busy design could well produce a claustrophobic sense of excess. But in the courtyard of Bou Inania it evokes a Zen-like calm. It is the ambition of Islamic art and architecture to illustrate the nature of God. And so in all that movement, in all those curvaceous swirling lines, there is a sense of stillness. And in the tremendous complexity of the designs, there is a wonderful simplicity. The courtyard becomes a place of repose, of refuge. In its tranquility, in its serenity, there is the sense of the divine, some echo of eternity.

In the Andalusian quarter of the medina I take lunch at Dar El Ghalia, an 18th century palace, now a kind of B&B owned by the Lebbar family. Fès is the birthplace of the pastille, the flaky pastry, light as rice paper, stuffed with minced pigeon, sugar, almonds, eggs and spices, and I lap it up like a fat bird.

After the lingering meal I venture outside the medina, where the late sunlight spreads over each object a sort of trembling, twilit dustiness. I make my way to the immense mechouar of the Royal Palace, with its crenellated roof and windows that wink blandly through white-trim, and am compelled to knock on the giant golden door (no answer). And then I jaunt a short way over to the Mellah, the Jewish quarter. Mellah is the word for salt. To Jews, who came to Morocco from Spain to escape the Inquisition, was relegated the task of salting and preserving the severed heads of the sultan's enemies (so they could be exhibited on walls as trophies of battle); and the area to which Jews, who paid a special tax for "protection," were consigned was called the *mellah*. The quarter is distinguished by the finely-carved lattice-work balconies that hang over the street....the Arab buildings have their balconies on the inside. Between the 12th and 16th centuries when the Jews were being chased out of Europe by the Inquisition, they needed a place to go, and Morocco opened its doors. It was a Kasbah of tolerance long before the rest of the world. Now the Mellah is distinguished by its gold shops, selling fine filigree necklaces, rings, even huge belts that belong in a World Wrestling championship, just adjacent to the synagogue.

That night, at dinner on a terrace of La Maison Bleu, the air seems taut with energy. Mohammed, the ever patient and tolerant driver, begins the meal with his usual entreaty, "Bis me lak," – "In the name of God," and as he mouths the phrase a flash of lightning storm strobes over the city.

It was on a terrace such as this that in 1912 the sultan signed the "Treaty of Fez" with France and Spain, which turned Morocco into a 'protectorate,' the stated aims of which were modernizing the country and preserving its traditions. To promote these fictions the sultan was retained as a figurehead. But European settlers prospered to the Moroccans detriment. The foreigners received the highest paying jobs and the best agricultural land; their children studied in schools while those of Moroccans did not. After 38 years of 'protection' only 15 percent of Moroccans had received any education at all, this in a land that housed colleges, libraries and scholars before the great learning institutions of Europe.

Tonight it seems we never order; rather we float, wanting for nothing. Salads arrive; roasted green pepper with cumin; artichokes and baby zucchini; cubed fried calf's liver; lamb and quince. There is a seven-vegetable couscous. Two waiters, in red jackets that fit as tightly as toreadors', carry a giant leather tajine and uncover it to reveal three whole chickens with lemons and olives. We eat it all with our fingers, and it is indeed finger-licking good.

16. HISTORY TAKES TIME

"Rusticus expectat, dum defluat amnis, at ille Labitur et labetur in omne volubilis aevum."

Translation:
"A rustic [peasant] waits on the shore
For the river to flow away,
But the river flows, and flows on as before,
And so it flows forever."
– Immanuel Kant, 1783

We take the night at the Jnan Palace Hotel, set in a seven-acre park, a retreat almost pious in its relative tranquility. As the sun mounts a pearly sky the day next Mohammed and I pile into his chariot and head north. We pass screens of sunflowers, herds of sheep (and a shepherd in a business suit tossing rocks and clucking at his flock), quilted valleys of olive groves, and we spy up on Mount Zerhoun, the holy city of Moulay Idriss, a whitewashed settlement that droops over the hills like a sleeping camel.

It is named for the country's first Muslim king, a descendant of the Prophet, and is also the site of his tomb. *Moulay* is a term roughly equivalent to "Saint." Moulay Idriss' reign was brief. He died in 792, said to have been poisoned under orders from Baghdad where Haroun al-Rashid—the caliph, or successor to the Prophet as the ruler of Islam—had grown jealous of the rival power that Idriss was developing.

Idriss' son, Moulay Idriss II, built the city from which we had just come, Fès, as Morocco's first Islamic capital.

Then we motor a few miles across a treeless alluvial plain, past wheat fields that have been under cultivation for nearly two thousand years, towards a site described by Edith Wharton in her guidebook to Morocco in 1925: "After a time we left oueds and villages behind us and were in the mountains of the Rarb, toiling across a high, sandy plateau. Far off a fringe of vegetation showed promise of shade and water, and at last, against a pale mass of olive-trees, we saw the sight which, at whatever end of the world one comes upon it, wakes the same sense of awe: the ruin of a Roman city."

We roll into the ghost of Volubilis, once the capital of the Roman province of Mauritania, at the westernmost border of the Roman Empire, and now, of course, as with any ruin of note, a World Heritage Site. Long abandoned, its excavation began less than 100 years ago, and it is now the largest and best preserved Roman ruin in the country. It was once overlorded by Juba II, a Roman-educated African who married the daughter of Marc Antony and Cleopatra. Juba was made king of Mauretania by the Romans in 25 BC. Less known is that Juba II was the author of botanical treatises in Greek, one of which discusses the medical uses of opium (it has been suggested that he anticipated the famous Moroccan *majoun,* a narcotic confection made with nuts, dried fruits, and cannabis...kif...a version of which scandalized Alice B Toklas's readers when she published a Moroccan-inspired recipe for hashish fudge, "which anyone could whip up on a rainy day.")

127

For Roman sensibilities this was a pleasing landscape, in both its fertility and shape, conforming to the notion of *amoenitas*: having gentle, decorous charm, being symmetrical and mild.

There had been a settlement on this spot since the Neolithic period. The Berbers built it into a significant outpost which they called Oulili, a corruption of *oaulili* (oleander), after the trees so generously scattered around the countryside here. Like any encampment, or shrub flowers, set far away there is both beauty and bitterness. The bitterness of the oleander plant is explained as having sprung from the tears of Fatima, the Prophet Mohammed's daughter, when she learned that she would have to share her husband, Ali, with a second wife.

Then, in the first century, the Romans arrived.

It's hard to do a mental dial-back and imagine this city 2000 years ago, milling and mixing with some 20,000 people, with a flourishing trade in oil (one house in four had an oil press), corn and wild animals such as panthers, elephants and gladiator-fighting lions for the Roman coliseums. Now it is populated mostly by bright blooming wild flowers… Volubilis is Latin for "morning glory."

To walk around the site today is a moving experience that brings both the grand achievements and daily routines of an ancient civilization vividly to life. The main paved street, the Decumonus Maximus, bisects the city from east to west. Axial roads were bordered by rows of large and richly decorated villas, of which many well preserved fragments remain. Especially notable are a series of faded mosaic floors that remain in situ depicting scenes from classical mythology and everyday life.

Executed in a mixture of black and white marble, red, orange and brown terracotta and blue and green glass, the mosaics retain their voluptuous, dazzling intensity, including one depicting the most un-Islamic of ancient gods, Dionysus, the god of wine.

The Muslim interdiction against portraying animals, birds, humans and flowers in art produces elaborate calligraphy and diamond-shaped mosaics and stucco fretwork, but little that might be called an aesthetic jolt…something out-of-the margins, random, fun or original in its creative expression. But here are dolphins sporting, a man riding a horse backward, a jolly squid, a witty prawn. On a stone block is a representation of an enormous phallus, perhaps three feet long. It marks the once luxurious bordello, which is now home only to nettles and scorpions.

The Decumonus is terminated by an imposing triumphal arch, built in 217 AD to honor the emperor Caracalla. Vestiges of the city's forum, basilica, temple, ramparts and bastions are also well preserved. The precise geometric and rhythmic repetitions of the grand design, down to the small pulsing tiles, are meant, some scholars believe, to invoke the order of the universe, to provide an antidote to the confusion of life. Volubilis, and of course the whole of the Roman empire, collapsed, whereas the chaos of the Kasbahs and the medinas of Morocco thrive today, almost as antidote to too much order.

I trek through a forest of columns, poking through the earth like giant dry bones. Most are topped with fat-tired stork nests, and their white-frocked architects clack when I get too close. I watch the Spanish sparrows disappear into these huge nests to create their own protected ones inside.

Scattered about are the remains of the olive oil presses that made Volubilis wealthy. Olive trees grow in the inky hills—and in profusion throughout much of Morocco—and olives and olive oil are as important to the Moroccan diet and the country's economy today as in Roman times.

After the Romans left, Volubilis was again occupied by Berber tribes and eventually abandoned in the ninth century, when the neighboring hilltop city of Moulay Idriss was founded. In the late 1600s the Sultan Moulay Ismail, known for his frequent arbitrary executions that marked his fifty-four year reign of terror, looted Volubilis for foundation stones to build the Imperial city of Meknes. In 1755 it was finally destroyed by shockwaves from the Lisbon earthquake. But an English antiquarian had made sketches there in 1722, which constituted a partial record. Moreover, the rubble contained some recognizable building remains, and a number of mosaics remained underneath them, facilitating restoration and reconstructions. French archeologists discovered the site and started excavation and rebuilding in World War I, working on the project with the aid of German prisoners. The Moroccan government has been digging here ever since.

In languid midday heat I watch the silent ruins, imagining trade and town life, noises and odors, the bread-and-circus of trade and work and leisure. This is the intrigue of ancient history, of imagining the unknowable.

17. MIND OVER CHATTER

"The first cup moistens my lips and throat. The second cup breaks my loneliness. The third cup searches my barren entrail but to find therein some thousand volumes of odd ideographs. The fourth cup raises a slight perspiration - all the wrongs of life pass out through my pores. At the fifth cup I am purified. The sixth cup calls me to the realms of the immortals. The seventh cup - ah, but I could take no more! I only feel the breath of the cool wind that raises in my sleeves. Where is Elysium? Let me ride on this sweet breeze and waft away thither"

-Lu Tung, during the T'ang Dynasty

"I got nasty habits; I take tea at three."
– Mick Jagger/Keith Richards, 1966

On the way out of Volubilis we thread up a hill and across a plain to penetrate the rammed-earth ramparts of the imperial city of Meknes. The 17th-century capital has 50 palaces, 20 gates, and 30 miles of walls, some of which were frankensteined from the ruins of Volubilis. Here I hope to catch up with Kristy Larson, who for fifteen years has been the Mountain Travel Sobek lead trekking guide in Morocco. She has been in-country for a total of 26 years, first in Essaouira as a Peace Corp volunteer, then in Marrakech making leather bags, and now as the only American living in Meknes. She is an avid equestrian, riding every day at the country's largest breeding farm, when not leading tours. Meknes is the horse capital of Morocco (founder Moulay Ismail reportedly kept 12,000 horses here).

Kristy has a cell phone….what American doesn't?….and when I reach and tell her Mohammed and I are lost in the Möbius strip of streets that is Meknes, she suggests we meet at one of her favorite haunts, a guest house in the middle of the ruins of the sultan's 17th century imperial palace, the Palais Didi, for some "Moroccan whiskey." Moulay Ismail emulated Louis XIV and built this palace on scale with Versailles, and he even hoped to add one of Louis's daughters to his harem of 500. The 15 miles of massive walls were supposedly built by Christian slaves and some 30,000 other prisoners, and there are rumors that some of the workers, who complained about the conditions, were walled in alive. After a quick tour of the subterranean vaults that housed up to 60,000 Christians captured by Barbary pirates, I'm ready for the offer of a local whiskey, and plop down across from Kristy.

But the spirit of the Kasbah here is not hooch….turns out "Moroccan Whiskey" is… tea.

Kristy explains: "Everyone in Morocco wants to host visitors and offer them something, and most frequently it is tea. Even with strangers…everywhere I go folks stop me and say come inside and have some tea. Even when I'm on horseback people come from their homes and beckon me for some tea."

Our waiter not so much walks as glides to us in his long white silk-embroidered cotton *gandoura,* carrying a silver engraved tray to our table, and begins the ritual of pouring and re-pouring the tea from the *berrad* to glass and back again, tossing in chunks of sugar and copious, aromatic sheaves of mint. Kristy tests it, and then nods to me. It is refreshing, if thick with sugar, and we both savor it.

"It's a fusion drink, like so much of the culture here. I believe the tea tradition began when Essaouira was the main trading port, and England brought the tea, which originated from China, to trade in the Kasbahs."

She is right. It stems from the Anglomania of the Jewish merchants of Mogador, who lived in the Kasbah, and were the exclusive importers of the precious leaves.

"You know so well the history here, and have the unusual perspective of a foreigner long in a foreign land. What is your definition of the Kasbah? I've heard a few so far," I venture after a satisfying slurp.

"The Kasbah is really a fortified house, a kind of castle, and a place for caravans to stay, and give the nomads shelter and safety. A passing of ideas and cultures happened here, and continues to this day. I walk out my apartment door and meet strangers every day, and pass back and forth conversation and ideas. I never feel lonely in this culture. I walk out my door and feel protected. In other countries it is hard to find someone to talk to. I feel safer in Morocco than in most places in the United States. People here take care of me. If I have a bag, someone always comes up and offers to carry it. People are always talking, talking, talking….if you are on a train and someone has a meal he shares it with everyone else. People love to share. I have never been to a place where it is so easy to meet new people. I have never seen a society that is as open as Morocco.

"When I first came here I really didn't know what to expect. I was surprised at how immediately safe I felt. I never was afraid. I traveled in buses and camels and horseback, and was always treated like family.

"I would recommend that you travel the whole of Morocco to meet the local people and get the spirit of the Kasbah."

18. TANGIER DREAM

"The fundamental delusion of humanity is to suppose that I am here and you are out there."
-Yasutani Roshi, Zen master, 1929

"There ain't no way to find out why a snorer can't hear himself snore"
-Samuel Langhorne Clemens, 1894

From Meknes we bore north, through layers and sub-layers of Morocco's underbelly, to Tangier. The one-time city of sin spreads its arms along the Straits of Gibraltar, where the blue of the Mediterranean meets the steel of the Atlantic. No African city is closer to Europe. "A dove poised on the shoulder of Africa," one poet put it. Waves of seafarers left their mark here: Phoenicians, Carthaginians, Romans. Berbers and Arabs settled in long-term, and the city was passed back and forth by the Spanish, Portuguese and English.

When Morocco was carved up by the colonial powers of France and Spain in the early 1920s, Tangier was given special status as an international free zone…that decadent status lasted until 1956. Loose tax laws and a free port attracted a community of dodgy business operators, and an atmosphere of moral permissiveness drew a demi-monde of writers, artists and general bon viveurs to the 'Interzone,' as William S. Burroughs dubbed it. It was a place you could pick up almost anything you wanted, and a quite a few you didn't.

But even before it's Free Zone status Tangier had a reputation for tolerance. It was here that Richard Burton arrived in December 1885, with his trunks of papers and books and his personal mission to translate the salacious epic *Arabian Nights.*

Part of the reason for Burton's visit to Morocco was to scope the country out. It had long been his dream to become the British ambassador, and the signs were good that his appointment was imminent. With twenty-five years of experience in the Consular Service, Burton had never been promoted, despite regarding the prime minister himself as a personal friend. He put his stalled diplomatic career down to a report he had written four decades earlier while in the employ of Sir Charles Napier, on a Karachi male brothel, touting a wide range of eunuchs and young boys.

Since no respectable British publisher would touch a translation of *Arabian Nights,* Burton arranged to mail each completed volume to a set of private subscribers. Still, his work leaked to the press, and one correspondent for the *Edinburgh Review* wrote: "Probably no European has ever gathered such an appalling collection of degrading customs and statistics of vice. It is a work which no decent gentleman will long permit to stand upon his shelves...Galland is for the nursery, Lane for the study, and Burton for the sewers."

Richard Burton never received his ambassadorship.

Inside the lobby of the graceful Hotel el Minzah the grandfather clock has stopped. This is a haunt that lists Winston Churchill, Rita Hayworth, Truman Capote and Ian Fleming among its former guests, and it looks as though little has changed since its celebrity heyday. Around the pool people are drinking, talking, gesturing…nobody on a cell phone or laptop, which is the default these days at American resorts. I pull out my BlackBerry to see if there is service, and it shows five bars…so the behavior here is elective.

Caid's Bar, down a flight from the lobby, looks familiar, and as I belly up and order a Mahia, a fig cognac, the barkeep tells me why…it was the inspiration for Rick's Café in Casablanca, he says. It was Tangier, not Casablanca, which was the international zone during the war, and where the spies and expatriates mingled. This was the inspiration for the story, and where Victor Lazlo would have fetched his transit papers.

We head down the Barbary Coast, foaming silver and white, to the Cape Spartel lighthouse, built in 1864 by Sultan Muhammad III, on the point of land closest to Spain. It's only 17 miles across the Strait of Gibraltar, and for years engineers, bankers, politopaths and visionaries have talked of building a trans-continental bridge. But to many it would mean the end of a separation that has served cultural preservation, and certain economics well, and the plans are on hold.

The first international convention ever signed by the United States, the 1865 Spartel Lighthouse Treaty, dealt with a navigational aid erected on the Moroccan side of the Strait of Gibraltar. The Treaty, ratified by Morocco, President Andrew Johnson and nine European heads of state, granted neutrality to the lighthouse with the condition that the ten naval powers signing the agreement assumed responsibility for its maintenance.

Past the venders selling leather belts, hats and purses; beyond the tables of stunning colored amethyst, pyrite and manganite, past the rock-roses and cork-oaks, a thousand feet down this promontory, the waters of the Mediterranean and the Atlantic converge and crash. Not a great crossing for swimmers, but not a problem for birds, and we see black kites, booted eagles and white storks flapping between the continents.

All sorts of boats have crashed into the rocks here, and more have passed by, including the most famous boat of all. Legend has it that after the deluge, Noah's ark drifted on. Close to Tangier, a bird came and landed on the bridge with a little clay on its claws. The occupants of the ark exclaimed then: "Tin jaa" ("The mud came") which means the land is near: hence the name Tangier. However, it is more likely that the name of the city comes from the Amazigh language, where the term "Tanja" designates a marsh.

Then we make our way southwest along the coast to Robinson Plage, a wide beach where kite-surfers are thrashing the waves, burkas mix with bikinis, teens are playing soccer on the sand, and old men are offering camel rides.

Tangier, and its environs, is more atmosphere, more myth, than real city. It's said that anyone can invent a story here and it will be believed. But perhaps the story with the greatest dramatic roughage plots around the Grottes d'Hercules (the Caves of Hercules), where the great man rested after having done his dozen deeds, according to Greek mythology. The limestone caves have been used as a dwelling since Neolithic times. Archaeological excavations have produced human bones and flints. Barbary Pirates hid here. For a long time locals quarried stone here. Then, in the first half of the 20th century, they were used as brothels, until it was discovered that tourists were a more lucrative venture.

We pass a life-size painting of Hercules unchained with arms raised high, muscles flexed, and then descend down a series of concrete steps into the grotto, lit with forty-watt bulbs that struggle to illuminate the gift shops. We peek out at the blue Atlantic through the famous hole, which is shaped eerily like Africa, but in reverse….there's even a hole floating off the lower edge of the continent that is Madagascar. It's easy to imagine here. It's easy to picture pirate ships running before the wind in the distance. Some people say that the caves were once joined under the sea to the St. Michaels caves on the rock of Gibraltar and that this is how the Barbary Apes crossed over.

The Greeks also have an explanation for the formation of Gibraltar. It was at the time of the titanic battle between the gigantic Antes and Hercules that Hercules opened Gibraltar with a sword stroke. Antes had in fact given the name of his wife "Tinga" to the region. Thereafter, Zeus's son raised two columns on both sides of the water that were going to carry the name of Heracles. For many centuries it was believed they designated the extremities of the earth. Tangier and the surrounding region was also the stomping ground of Odysseus, hero of the famous *Odyssey* of Homer.

Just a giant's step from the Caves of Hercules are the Ruins of Lixus. Here, the mythology muses, Hercules accomplished the

11th of his 12 labors, stealing the golden apples that grew in the Garden of the Hesperides on Mount Atlas. Hercules asked Atlas to gather the fruit while he supported the sky on his shoulders.

A short ways south we pass around the King's beach house, where he often relaxes and takes his jet ski out for a ride. Mohammed says the King once was scooting about and came across a windsurfer who had been knocked into the water and was close to drowning. The King pulled him onto the royal jet ski, and saved the sportsman.

Adjacent to the king's compound is the ancient Roman site of Cotta, a small area of stone ruins set among a field of daises just above the beach. The archeological excavations have revealed several wall sections and the layout of a Roman town, probably dating from the 2nd and 3rd centuries.

It's not nearly as spectacular as Volubilis, but it has no tourists, so it is a peaceful thrill to wander about the mixture of villa and Roman industrial complex, with its baths, temples, shrine, oil press and central courtyard lined with huge cemented vats used for salting fish and processing oil and the other products of the town.

Like many of the classical sites on the Moroccan coast, Cotta specialized in the manufacture of the rancid sauce made from fish guts called Garum (anchovy paste) that was beloved by the Romans. This to me seems a more likely cause for the fall of the empire than lead in the cups, but then I am one to always hold the anchovies.

After a lunch break, we head further south to a bite-sized town that hugs like a white dream to the edge of Morocco...

Asilah. Its known origins trace back to 1,500 BC, when it was a trade center for the Phoenicians, and it has enjoyed a ping-pong game of possession since. In 1471 the Portuguese occupied Asilah. Then in 1578, after the Battle of the Three Kings, it became a Spanish possession. It returned to Moroccan hands in 1589, but then in 1911 the Spaniards reoccupied the city, and it remained part of Spanish Morocco until it was returned to the Moroccan kingdom in 1956. In parts of the last two centuries it was also used by pirates as a home base. It has always been connected to Europe in some fashion, and now literarally it has a French Connection, with the completion in 2007 of an undersea telecommunications cable that links it directly to Marseille, France.

Today Asilah is most famous for its annual festival of arts, culture and thought, the Cultural Moussem of Asilah. Founded in 1978 by former Moroccan Minister of Foreign Affairs and ambassador to the U.S., Mohamed Benaissa, the summer-long festival invites musicians, dancers, theater troupes and visual artists from all over the world for performances and workshops. Visual artists splash the walls of Asilah's medina with wild murals, so it is now somewhat of an outdoor art gallery. The festival's success brought an overhaul of Asilah's infrastructure, and restoration of 60 per cent of its buildings; the town was designated a National Monument and, in 1989, received the Aga Khan Award for Architecture.

Last year TripAdvisor.com, a travel web site owned by Expedia, the company I worked for when it launched as a

Microsoft product in 1996, surveyed more than 2,500 travelers globally, finding the top trends were concerns about germs, the growth of green tourism, and opposition to cell phone use while traveling. Among the top ten emerging destinations in the survey was Asilah. It certainly is gorgeous. I ease among old Portuguese ramparts that straddle the rocks, past the white-washed walls, many festooned with murals, by a Gnawa musician in a cap trimmed with cowry shells singing for his supper, and by the sparkling blue doorways, most no taller than a barrel.

I head back to Tangier for the night, and while winding along the coast road The Song crashes around my head: "Looking at the world through the sunset in your eyes. Traveling the train through clear Moroccan skies" —Marrakesh Express by Crosby, Stills and Nash was one of the defining songs of the hippie era, a paean to adventure and travel, and it inspired me. This was a song that not only made me want to hit the road, it instructed where to go. I was 19 when I first heard its exhortation to "take the train from Casablanca heading south." It has been a theme to my travels ever since.

We all follow in someone's footsteps. Graham Nash, co-author of the song "Marrakesh Express," was himself emulating the members of the Beat Generation - William Burroughs, Jack Kerouac, Allen Ginsberg - who in the 1950s had made a playground out of Tangier where the railway line to Marrakech begins.

In those days Tangier had its own laws and administration, more than 60,000 expats and a hundred brothels. Burroughs boasted that he received "an average of 10 attractive propositions a day," mostly from young boys. But it didn't last. Moroccan independence in 1956 followed by a series of scandals brought an end to Tangier's days of excess, but not to its font of creativity.

19. THE WILD, WILD WESTON

"Night is gone—
I hear your song,
African lady.
The dark fades away,
Now it's day.
A new morning breaks.
The birds in the sky all sing
For Africa awakes.
Bright light floods the land,
And Tomorrow's in your hand.
African lady."
– Langston Hughes, 1960

Tangier is still a draw for artists of all stripes, and it is in Tangier, in the lobby of the Mövenpick Hotel & Casino, a relatively new edifice on the seaside Corniche, that I run into one of my musical heroes, Randy Weston. Born in 1926, six-foot-eight inches tall in his corduroy baseball cap, Randy was the pioneer pianist who was among the first to fuse classic American jazz with African rhythms and tonalities. He was World Beat before the term existed. He is back visiting the city he called home for an influential stint in his career.

Randy was born and grew up in the Bedford-Stuyvesant section of Brooklyn, where his father, the owner of a soul food diner, emphasized to his son, "You are an African born in America." The elder Weston laid down a strict rule for Randy: Practice the piano at home each day or feel the edge of a ruler on your knuckles. When Randy was in his early teens he was already six- feet-two-inches tall and eager to play basketball, but his dad ensured he didn't stray too far from his piano. Passing along his knowledge and appreciation of calypso, jazz, and blues on to his son, Randy's dad frequently took him to see Duke Ellington when playing in town. In addition, Weston's mother, who was from Virginia, exposed her young son to spirituals. "I had a great father. I had a wonderful father. He always told me as a boy Africa was our ancestral home, and we have to know the history of who we are. Before he died, I brought my dad to Tangier."

While Randy was growing up in Brooklyn in the 1930s and 1940s Miles Davis, Max Roach, and George Russell all lived in the borough, and each stopped into his Dad's luncheonette for soul food. Randy felt steeped in the African American music community as a teenager; he especially made a point of seeing Coleman Hawkins perform whenever possible, and through Hawkins, he met Thelonious Monk. "He played like they must have played in Africa 5000 years ago," he tells me.

At age 14 Randy was taught by drummer Al Harewood how to play a tune on the piano by ear. He was soon able to imitate current releases by Ellington, Hawkins, and Count Basie. Weston used to go to the Atlantic Avenue section of Brooklyn to hear Arabic musicians play the oud. "We were searching for new sounds. We'd get into quarter and eighth tones. But here was

Monk doing it, with spirit power, with magic!... For me it was pure African piano."

Voted "new star pianist" in a 1955 Down Beat critics' poll, Randy spent most of the 1950s playing in clubs around New York City. He also toured colleges with historian Marshall Stearns, who lectured while Weston and a few other musicians performed African, calypso, Dixieland, and bebop music. He wrote a string of popular songs, including "Saucer Eyes," "Pam's Waltz," "Little Niles," and his best-known tune, "Hi-Fly," which is about being six-foot-eight and looking at the ground.

In 1960 Randy recorded Uhuru Africa, featuring narration by writer Langston Hughes, and African traditional styles with a jazz orchestra.

In 1961 Randy made his first trip to Africa by way of a festival aimed at exchanging Black American ideas and music with those of Africans. Then in 1966, Randy visited 14 African countries while on a U.S. State Department tour, and of all the places he saw and felt and heard throughout the continent, Tangier was the place that sang loudest to him, and he decided to settle here. He didn't know the culture or the chief languages, but he spoke music, and felt at home in Morocco. He owned a nightclub downtown from 1968 until 1972, and he wrote his classic Tangier Bay in 1970, in praise of the beauty he saw from his house on a hill. "The colors were so brilliant, it was like a movie" he remembers.

The club went bankrupt...he was better at music than business, so he left Tangier and lived in Europe and America, but returned to Africa whenever he could.

The 1980s saw Randy receive recognition for his original style of blending cultures in his music with a raft of awards and tributes, and documentaries such as "Randy in Tangiers," which closes with Randy playing in a Kasbah (and Paul Bowles is there, too) and "African Rhythms" for PBS.

At the close of the 1980s Randy released "Portraits," a Moroccan-Arabic-jazz fusion that I often played on my Walkman, and listened to its steps as I made my way up Mount Kilimanjaro.

In the 1990s Randy went on tour with a Moroccan Gnawa group, and played through North and West Africa. In 1992 he released another album, "Spirits of Our Ancestors," underscoring the African link between forms of modern-day American music and featuring musicians Melba Liston, Pharoah Sanders, Dizzy Gillespie, and Dewey Redman. In 1995, he released "The Splendid Master Musicians of Morocco and Marrakesh: In the Cool of the Evening."

Sitting on some lobby chairs by the busy elevator (nobody recognizes the legend) I ask Randy about the origins of his music.

"There cannot be a civilization without music. Just imagine one day if all the music stopped in the world. The planet would die. Music is our spiritual language.

"All music comes from Africa. Africa holds our oldest civilization. The whole concept of music came from the ancients who were in tune with the universe. They were in tune with the animals, the insects the planets. Mother Nature was the first orchestra. Traditional music has the language of Mother Nature, something we in the West have gotten away from.

"When I first heard Gnawa music at a traditional ceremony here I heard the black church, I heard the blues and jazz all at the same time. It was like going back to the origins of music. It was like going back to my great, great, great, great grandfather. I went wow! This is the music.

"Gnawa is the music of ancestors. The Gnawans play games with their music; they call certain spirits with music; they heal with music. Every note has a meaning. This music is the past, present and future. All the rhythms we have in the West—whether we call it Rock & Roll, whether we call it pop; whether we call it hip-hop—if you take out the rhythms and the spirituality from Africa, you have nothing. The beauty of this music is that when we listen we become one…there is no separation among the audience…we are one human family.

"I discovered the strings of Africa….everyone thinks of the drums, but hearing the strings was like coming back home. We have a lot to learn from our ancestors. There is a magic to it. People here can make music from anything…from a bottle, a table, from the feet, or the chest, while on a camel or a horse. Music here is life itself.

"The spirit of the Kasbah is magic. It's about spirituality. If they only have one loaf of bread Moroccans are going to share a slice with you. This is the spiritual center of our planet."

Randy than offers to play a riff for me. "I love playing here. Moroccans love music so much. This is the only country I've been to where the hotel staff doesn't ask for a tip—they ask for a cassette of my music."

Randy then takes his long strides…there is a lupine elegance to his walk… to the lobby lounge, pushes open the cover of the black Yamaha piano, and as he sits I get to say a variation of a phrase that I have oft hoped to be able to say in Morocco: "Play it again, Randy."

His long fingers begin to fly around the ivories, and he magics a song with Gnawa roots….it is magic, and those around us look up from their coffee and newspapers and listen, as though touched by an angel, not knowing who the pianist is, but feeling they are in the presence of something magical and great.

"Music can open up many, many doors," he grins.

20. A NEGATION OF TIME

"I refute it thus."
– Samuel Johnson, 1763, contesting Bishop Berkeley's philosophical view that the external, physical world does not exist and is a product of the mind

Later that day I head over to the terrace of the Café Hafa, the little cliff-side tea house hanging above the Mediterranean where Paul Bowles, Tennessee Williams, Samuel Becket, Eugène Delacroix, Henri Matisse, Timothy Leary and Jean Genet once sat and sipped and did their intellectual whankings. My driver Mohammed says that Jane Bowles, Paul's wife, was poisoned to death here in 1973 by her love-struck housekeeper.

I settle into a white plastic chair beneath a cane trellis of hanging grapes and sit and sip some sweet mint tea, beneath a soundtrack of birdsong. A sea breeze blows the steam off my tea, and I settle back to contemplate… but no inspiration arrives…just a peaceful feeling that it would not be the worst thing to just chuck it all and move here and watch the waters and the sun and move to the leisurely rhythms of this place. A ship's horn sounds dully in the distance. The ritual of sipping tea, I recognize, denies our faith in evolutionary progress, and returns us to our primordial roots.

Then I venture into the medina of Tangier, dominated by a minaret in multicolored faience that rises above the Sidi Bou Abid mosque. It looks lonely here. It evokes a holy place, but Tangier for a spell was considered anything but. Just half a century back Tangier was considered among the most deliciously decadent cities in the world. The medina was the notorious Interzone in William Burroughs' classic book, *Naked Lunch*.

Many things have changed since then. Morocco found its independence and tucked Tangier into its fold, so it now has the rule of society and monarchy. It is spicy still, and bursting with movement and color, but the sin is no longer in blatant showcase. What is the same is the simmering stew of human life…folks of all stripes passing, laughing, bartering, philosophizing, gossiping…it is a labyrinthine river of people and their ideas and passions and goods. It lives every moment in a swirling universe of undying thoughts and inspirations.

Just outside the medina, through a high archway, and on a visible slope, is a large roundabout with a huge gaudy fountain in the center, ringed with palm trees. This is The Grand Socco (The Great Souk) or Place du 9 avril 1947. It was in this square, on April 9th 1947, that sultan Mohammed V made a famous speech in which he referred to independence for Morocco. It was not always so righteous. When Richard Burton was ensconced in a nearby hotel in 1885 feverishly translating *Arabian Nights* he often walked this square. His description: "It is a foul slope; now slippery with viscous mud, then powdery with fetid dust, dotted with graves and decaying tombs, unclean booths, gargotes and tattered tents, and frequented by women, mere bundles of unclean rags…"

I stop and watch the people gather and intersect and reflect and play and then move on. It is like a river of fluid ties, of both intimate and casual encounters. Several strangers stop and say hello, or ask if I am lost, or where I am from; some nod and smile as they pass by. I pull the scene through the machinery of my mind. What's different about this gathering place? I look around and try to assimilate what I see....but then I recognize that it is what I don't see that is different. There are no iPhones or BlackBerries or any digital devices in evidence. There are no electronic walls. People come here to actually meet; to converse; to engage and exchange real ideas. There are no lonely crowds here.

Standing here, in a place once legend for its political and social tyranny, it seems the old tyranny of place could become a new tyranny of time, as nomads who are "always on" all too often end up—mentally—anywhere but here (wherever here may be). As for friends and family, permanent mobile connectivity might have the same effect as nomadism: it might bring one much closer to family and friends, but it may make it harder to bring in outsiders. It might isolate cliques. My undergraduate degree is in Sociology from Northwestern University, and I still pal around with sociologists, and some fret about constant e-mailers and texters losing the everyday connections to casual acquaintances or strangers who may be sitting next to them in the café or on the bus. That is a current dynamic in the western world; but not yet here. It could be said that we in the West are now, more than ever before, building barricades with our devices, employing screens that screen out strangers. Yes, they reinforce family and friends—we can chat and text and twitter with them more than ever—yet we are blocking the chance encounters, the random meetings, and with them the brushes against novel and unfamiliar perspectives, and the shivery flashes of insights. Morocco was and is different, and its Kasbahs disarm all who enter.

The tools of modern nomadism clearly bring families closer by allowing them to stay connected when physically separated. But there are unexpected side effects in many everyday situations. It was not long ago that a leak appeared in the pan beneath the shower in my upper-floor master bedroom, and water began to drip through the ceiling of my kitchen. So I called a plumber, who promised to stop by. A few hours later I was standing on my porch saying goodbye to guests when the plumber walked up the stairs, past me and my departing guests, and into the house, with a cell phone pressed against his ear. He later apologized and said he was in a deep conversation with his wife, and was so intent on her words he missed the usual protocols of visitation.

Here was an example of two big tensions in nomadic society. First, mobile technology pitted the plumber's interaction with a stranger, me, against that with his own wife on the phone. The plumber, to use the technical term, had a "weak tie" to me, but a "strong tie" to his wife, which easily prevailed over the weak one, leaving me and my friends feeling temporarily awkward, and pondering the fate of society.

Second, the plumber gave precedence to the "mediated" interaction with the person at the other end of the phone, at the expense of his "co-present" communication with me, who was standing right next to him. In other words, the person who was physically more distant was nonetheless psychologically closer. So out went social norms and rituals (handshakes, greetings) that Western societies accumulated during a past of exclusively co-present interactions.

Sociologists argue about the precise role of ritual in society and the relative importance of the individual, family and community. Emile Durkheim kicked off the debate more than a century ago when he studied Australian aborigines and found they used rituals to create and maintain solidarity and cohesion among a group. In the 1950s Erving Goffman broadened the definition of rituals to ordinary interactions of daily American life, such as jokes. Here in Morocco, Islam (which translates as 'submission'—to the will of God) celebrates the observance of ritual, such as the five-times-a-day call to prayer. In the concept of *Umma*, the Islamic Nation, is a rebuttal of Western Individualism, and an antidote to loneliness and alienation.

In the 1970s Mark Granovetter became an influential sociologist with a paper titled "The Strength of Weak Ties". He argued that society needs not only healthy "strong ties" between relatives and friends but also ample and fluid "weak ties" between casual acquaintances. Far from trivial, these weak ties are the "bridges" between "densely knit clumps of close friends" and thus the conduits for ideas, fads and trends. "Social systems lacking in weak ties will be fragmented and incoherent," Mr. Granovetter argued. Any erosion of weak ties is therefore to be deplored.

A NEGATION OF TIME

In the 1990s, as the internet came into widespread use, sociologists, never an upbeat bunch to begin with, became decidedly pessimistic. Some observed a "loss of social capital" as people spent their time transfixed by screens rather than other people. Others saw the real-world (as opposed to online) social networks of Americans shrinking, with ever more people feeling that they were intimate with nobody at all. Robert Kraut at Carnegie Mellon University argued that the internet causes social isolation and depression. Norman Nie at Stanford University believed that "internet use at home has a strong negative impact on time spent with friends and family as well as time spent on social activities."

But most of these observations, made in a rich country at the height of the PC era, focused on the wired and stationary kind of communications technology rather than the wireless and mobile sort. Now, as more of us worship at the church of mobile communications, a new generation of sociologists is scrambling to update all these theories. So far, most of them agree that nomadic technology, far from isolating people, brings them closer to their families, friends and lovers—their strong ties. But they still disagree on what that means for weak ties with strangers, and thus western society at large.

Nomadic technology deepens family ties because, as another sociologist, Christian Licoppe, puts it, it enables "connected presence," which is new in history. In the era of stationary communications technology, people used landline phones that belonged to a place rather than a person. In that communication culture people talked infrequently and viewed a conversation as an occasion. Typically, they would plan the call for an appropriate time, such as a Sunday. For most of my adult life I called my mother on Sunday evenings. We often didn't have much to say, but we honored the ritual, and took the time to connect and catch up.

With cell phones, on the other hand, people call, text or e-mail one another constantly throughout the day. Since they are always, in effect, contacting a person rather than a place, and since the receiver can see the caller's name, and sometimes his picture, they often dispense with greetings altogether. The exchanges now tend to be frequent and short. People expect less content but instead a feeling of permanent connection, as though they were in fact together during the entire time between their physical meetings.

While recently in Norway I came across a study conducted in Oslo that found that about half of all cell phone calls and text messages go to the same three or four people, typically within six miles of the caller. A lot of this is "micro-co-ordination," as family members are out about town and check in with each other to plan their next stop or errand. Back in California I do this all the time....I call from my bike if I am wheeling late; my son Walker emails the name of the latest videogame he wants me to pick up.

But such communications go far beyond the merely utilitarian. Manuel Castells, the sociologist at the University of Southern California's Annenberg School for Communication (where I went to graduate school and picked up a masters in communications), says that mobile technology affects children the most. On one hand, adolescents today become socially autonomous earlier than their parents did, "building their own communities from the bottom up" through constant text-messaging and photo-sharing among their clique, even if this circumvents the wishes of parents. On the other hand, they also have their parents on speed-dial, and are only one button away from help if they get into trouble. Mr. Castells calls this a "safe autonomy pattern".

This has some sociologists concerned. James Katz at Rutgers calls the cell phone a new sort of umbilical cord between children and their parents and wonders whether this might in some cases "retard maturation". Sherry Turkle, a psychologist at MIT, says that wireless gadgets are, ironically, a "tethering technology" and create new dependencies that delay the important "Huck Finn moment" in young lives when adolescents first realize that they are alone on the urban equivalent of the Mississippi. Getting drunk and lost after a party is different when one push of a button summons the parental chauffeur. The argument is often made about adventurers….it's not the same if you can call for help on the mountain if the weather turns bad. Or if you get lost in the Moroccan desert in a sandstorm. In 2005, a psychology professor at Middlebury College in Vermont found that undergraduates were communicating with their parents, on average, more than ten times a week.

Often entire cliques do this sort of thing, creating, in effect, their own tribal medium and narrative. People now use their phones to snap photos of everyday situations—the view from the porch on a rainy day—which may mean a lot to a friend or family member, but nothing to anybody else.

The potential problem with connected presence is that it usually excludes other people who may be physically present. In situations that might once have been an opportunity to talk to a stranger—waiting for a coffee or cup of tea, or boarding an airplane, say—people now fill the time with a few messages to parents, lovers or friends. This strengthens the strong ties, but weakens or even cuts the weak ties in society. In some cases it leads to "bounded solidarity," when cliques become so turned in on themselves that they all but stop interacting with the wider society around them. It is the anti-Kasbah, in that it shuts out travelers and strangers. It is the opposite of the open way that Morocco is going.

The first casualty of this new nomadism is usually etiquette. Noise pollution is only one kind of violation. In a survey conducted in 2005, 62% of the people polled—and 74% of those over 60—felt that "using a cell phone in public is a major irritation for other people," but only 32% of those between 18 and 27 shared that opinion. That divergence makes for a combustible social cocktail whenever the generations mix. It is habit nowadays for westerners to answer calls in movie theaters, restaurants and public toilets, even at weddings and funerals. The volume of these transgressions varies with the culture—as around the bar, Americans and Italians are louder than Swedes or Japanese. Morocco just motors along as it always has, putting a premium on real social contact, not on mobile technology (though it of course exists, it has not subsumed tradition by any stretch). The oral tradition in Morocco is perfected and sleek, like stones in a river rounded by time.

Trickier etiquette problems arise when the issue is not so much noise as context. One example that will enter the history books occurred in September 2007 when Rudy Giuliani was waging his vigorous campaign for the presidency. As he was up on his podium and in mid-sentence addressing the National Rifle Association (NRA), a crucial constituency for a Republican candidate, his cell phone rang and, to gasps in the huge audience, he decided to answer it. What followed, captured on microphone, is worth repeating in its banality: "Hello, dear. I'm talking, I'm talking to the members of the NRA right now. Would you like to say hello? I love you, and I'll give you a call as soon as I'm finished. OK? OK, have a safe trip. Bye-bye. Talk to you later, dear. I love you." When he hung up, the audience had turned to stone.

Usually the situation is subtler and the incongruence has more to do with attention. This can be true even during silent cell communications. It's now routine for Western university students to text, e-mail, twitter and instant-message during lectures. In every airport in America through which I pass I see people hunched down, plowing their own furrow through the terminal, all the while emailing and texting. It's an atomized and individualized scene: a new form of the proverbial lonely crowd.

The spread of "hands-free" Bluetooth devices, with hidden earplugs seemingly attached to nothing, is removing even the clues of closed communications. Recently I was traveling on The Glacier Express in Switzerland when a girl standing next to me started talking to me. She asked me how I was and how my day had been. I was delighted a stranger would ask me this, and I started to answer that I was looking forward to seeing the Matterhorn when she gave me a black-eyed look of disgust and then turned away. Then I heard her say, "OK, I'll call you later" into her Bluetooth. Not a word or gesture was exchanged between us for the rest of journey.

Probably the single most common etiquette conflict occurs when mediated communication interrupts co-present communication, as when two or more people are sitting at a table in conversation or negotiation and one of them gets, and answers, a call. The other co-present people must now keep themselves busy while seeming nonchalant. What is more, they must pretend not to be eavesdropping even though they are only a few feet away from the mediated conversation, ideally by assuming a pose of concentration on some other object, such as fingernails or their own phone. As soon as the intervening call ends, everybody must try to re-enter the co-present context as gracefully as possible.

So there is evidence that nomadism is good for in-groups, but at the expense of strangers. If that is true, I consider it bad for society. Fortunately, however, the last chapter has not yet been written. Since the outburst of pessimism about the internet among sociologists in the 1990s, the web has recently become an intensely social medium, thanks in large part to proliferating online social networks such as Facebook and MySpace. People have been using these websites to keep in touch with much larger groups of people than has ever before been feasible. I am not immune. It is not uncommon for me to add several "friends" a day to my "social graph" on LinkedIn and Plaxo. And recently when my friend, the modern explorer Pasquale Scaturro, had a relapse of malaria while in Namibia, it was through a Facebook page that I was able to communicate with his daughter and keep up with his status.

As mobile devices now become, in effect, computers for accessing the wider web, these online services are also moving from stationary to mobile use. Whether that can re-invigorate the weak ties in western society along with the strong ties remains to be seen. But what differentiates Morocco from this madding crowd is a deep respect and celebration of tradition, and a tradition, from the days of the Kasbahs, that invites strangers into the conversation. The chain of transmission here is made through generations of accumulated conversation.

21. SILENCE IS THE DOOR OF CONSENT

"A good traveler is one who does not know where he is going to,
and a perfect traveler does not know where he came from"
– Lyn Yutang, 1965

When technology shifts, it bends the culture. But sometimes this turn is hard to spot precisely because it hides in plain sight. It is such with wireless communications. Something that people think of as just another technology is showing signs of changing lives, religion, politics, cities, jobs, even marriages dramatically. In particular, it will usher in a new version of a very old idea: nomadism.

After a board meeting at Mountain Travel Sobek in Emeryville, California, I sometimes head over to the nearby Nomad Café in Oakland and order a latte. I would sit, my brew next to my BlackBerry and Kindle, open my HP laptop and log on to the café's wireless internet connection to check email, research on the web, and write. Permanently connected, I communicate by text, photo, video or voice throughout the day with my friends and family, while working at the same time. This is true for me around the world, even in Morocco....I roam around the world, but often alight at oases that cater to nomads.

The idea behind these cafés is to provide watering-holes for "techno-Bedouins" such as myself. Since Bedouins, whether in the Moroccan deserts or American suburbs, are inherently tribal and social creatures, from the outset the goal is to create a good oasis. It has to do more than provide Wi-Fi; it must also become a new—or very old—kind of gathering place.

As a word, vision and goal, modern urban nomadism has had the mixed blessing of a premature debut. In the 1960s and 70s Marshall McLuhan, the media and communications theorist, pictured nomads zipping around at great speed, using facilities on the road and all but dispensing with their homes. In the 1980s Jacques Attali, a French economist who was advising President François Mitterrand at the time, used the term to predict an age when rich and uprooted elites would jet around the world in search of fun and opportunity, and poor but equally uprooted workers would migrate in search of a living. In the 1990s Tsugio Makimoto and David Manners jointly wrote the first book with "digital nomad" in the title, adding the bewildering possibilities of the latest gadgets to the vision.

But all of those early depictions and predictions of nomadism arguably missed the point. The mobile lifestyles currently taking shape around the world are nothing like those described in the old Moroccan books. The authors can't be blamed, since the underlying technologies of genuine and everyday nomadism didn't exist even as recently as a decade ago. Cell phones were already widespread, but they were used almost exclusively for voice calls and were fiendishly hard to connect to the internet and even to computers. Laptop computers and PDAs needed fiddly cables to get online, and even then did so at a snail's pace. Reading and sending e-mail on a cell phone—not to mention synchronizing it across several gadgets and computers to create one "virtual" in-box—was unheard of. People took photos using film. There was no Wi-Fi. In short, there were gadgets, but precious little "connectivity."

Without that missing piece, several misunderstandings took hold that now require correcting. One had to do with all those gadgets. The old mental picture of a nomad invariably had him—mostly him, at that time—lugging lots of them. Since these machines, large and small, were portable, people assumed that they also made their owners mobile. Not so. The proper metaphor for somebody who carries portable but unwieldy and cumbersome infrastructure is that of an astronaut rather than a nomad. Astronauts must bring what they need, including oxygen, because they cannot rely on their environment to provide it. They are both defined and limited by their gear and supplies.

Around the turn of the century, as some astronauts, western travelers and road warriors got smarter about packing light…the Berber always only took what could be carried on a camel's back. They graduated to an intermediate stage, becoming hermit crabs, the crustaceans that survive by dragging around a cast-off mollusk shell for protection and shelter. In the metaphorical sense, the shell might be a "carry-on" bag on wheels, stuffed full of cables, disks, dongles, batteries, plugs and paper documents (just in case of disk failure). I was one such road warrior when I worked for Microsoft. More than once I struck fear into the hearts of seated airline passengers as I banged down the aisle on the way to my seat.

Urban nomads have started appearing only in the past few years. Like their antecedents in the Moroccan desert, they are defined not by what they carry but by what they leave behind, knowing that the environment will provide it. Thus, Bedouins do not carry their own water, because they know where the oases are. Modern nomads carry almost no paper because they access their documents on their laptop computers, cell phones or online. Increasingly, they don't even bring laptops. Many engineers at Microsoft travel with only a BlackBerry or other "smart phones." If ever the need arises for a large keyboard and some earnest typing, they sit down in front of the nearest available computer anywhere in the world, open its web browser and access all their documents online. I do this all the time.

Another big misunderstanding of previous decades was to confuse nomadism with migration or travel. As the costs of (stationary) telecommunications plummeted, it became fascinating to contemplate the death of distance, or the killing of "the tyranny of geography," as my friend Nathan Myhrvold, then the Chief Technology Officer at Microsoft, used to say. And since the early cell phones were aimed largely at business executives, it was assumed that nomadism was about corporate travel in particular. And indeed many nomads are frequent flyers, for example, which is why several airlines have introduced in-flight Wi-Fi (thankfully, not Royal Air Maroc). But although nomadism and travel can coincide, they need not.

Humans have always migrated and travelled, without necessarily living nomadic lives. The nomadism now emerging is different from, and involves much more than, merely making journeys. A modern nomad is as likely to be a teenager in Los Angeles, Seattle, or Oslo as a jet-setting chief executive. He or she may never have left his or her city, stepped into an airplane or changed address. Indeed, how far he moves is completely irrelevant. Even if an urban nomad confines himself to a small perimeter, he nonetheless has a new and surprisingly different relationship to time, to place and to other people. Permanent connectivity, not motion, is the critical thing. Nomadism tends to bring people who are already close, such as family members, even closer. But it does so at the expense of attentiveness towards strangers encountered physically (rather than virtually) in daily life. We may be wrapped in an invisible web and neutralized with its juices.

Anthropologists and sociologists are investigating how mobile and virtual interaction spices up or challenges physical and offline chemistry, and whether it makes young people in particular more autonomous or more dependent. Architects, property developers and urban planners are changing their thinking about buildings and cities to accommodate the new habits of the nomads that dwell in them. Activists are trying to piggyback on the ubiquity of nomadic tools to improve the world, even as they worry about the same tools in the hands of the malicious. Linguists are chronicling how nomadic communication changes language itself, and thus thought.

But where are the random human connections in all this, such as those I see here on this square? Since humans, as Sigmund

Freud put it, must *arbeiten und lieben*, work and love, in order to find fulfillment, can we look to Morocco and its braided past and present to find a meaningful path to the future?

Futurology is a dangerous business, but the social changes are already visible: parents on the beaches of Marina del Rey waving at their children while typing furtively on their BlackBerrys; entrepreneurs discovering they don't need offices after all (if you need to recharge something just head to Starbucks); teen girls text-dumping their boyfriends. Everybody in the West is doing more on the move.

The ancient nomads of Morocco went from place to place—and they had to take a lot of stuff with them (including their livelihoods and families). The emerging class of digital nomads also wander, but they take virtually nothing with them; wherever they go, they can easily reach people and information. And the barriers to entry are falling. You don't have to be rich to be a nomad (I am evidence). It is getting harder to find places that don't have internet connectivity or cell service. I've phoned home from the tops of mountains, while floating down deep-canyoned rivers, while sailing on the ocean, even from deep in the Libyan Desert.

Back in 1996 I organized and led an expedition to make the first descent of the Tekeze River in Ethiopia, running through the deepest gorge in Africa, half a mile deeper than the Grand Canyon of the Colorado. On that trip I took a raft of communications gear so as to post blogs, with audio and video, every day as the expedition unfolded. Several on the trip decried the exercise as the death of wilderness. I may have been contributing to a type of nomadism that has unhealthy aspects, but I didn't see it as killing the rough country.

When the late Ed Hillary spoke out against commercial climbs up Everest, his words rang with remorse for a season lost to time: "How thankful I was that I was active in a pioneering era when we established the route, carried the loads, all worked together for the ultimate objective. The way things are now, I don't think I would have bothered." Even before the Tekeze expedition, the same was being said about the appearance of the Internet on remote expeditions: that it somehow diminished the experience, and those who climbed a mountain or ran an unrun river before the advent of GPSs and connections to the Web were the real pioneers, with a much more authentic adventure. Many have complained that Yosemite, the Grand Canyon, Kilimanjaro and Victoria Falls have lost some transcendence because of their manufactured and commercial accessibility, and that the backcountry is no longer so if one can call for help on a cell phone. Some argue, however, it is elitist to deny others what you have experienced, to preserve in private sanctuary the epiphany that came with a special effort, time and place. In my years as a river guide I escorted blind children, senior citizens, and paraplegics down the Colorado River, and I can testify that the transformational aspects of the experience were as vital for them as for the young, hearty do-it-yourself expeditioneers. It may be less of a feat now to climb Everest than in 1953, what with better gear, communications technology, and routes well described, but is the adventure really less, for the guides, for the clients, who feel the same elation and sense of personal achievement on top?

Forty years ago Dr. Rod Nash published *Wilderness and the American Mind*, a seminal work that explored the evolution of thought and behavior towards wilderness in the New World, from the European settlers, who viewed nature as something to be subdued, to today's urban romantics, who revere places that have escaped the human tap. In November 1995 I invited Rod to a demonstration of TerraQuest and its "virtual expedition" to Antarctica, in which a team I put together explored the edges of the White Continent and uplinked daily to a website, sending digital images, sounds and dispatches to the wired world, as well as answering e-mail and engaging in Live Chats. "This is the death of wilderness," Rod proclaimed after the demo. Before that, in the summer of the same year, when I brought a couple of digital cameras and a satellite communications system on a float trip down the San Juan River in the Four Corners Region, several members of the party told me they considered canceling when they heard of the high-tech element, because they felt it would compromise the wilderness they loved and remembered from past trips. One called my project "a spiritual invasion of time set aside to explore one's soul," and compared the Internet in the wilderness to "a brass band running through a cemetery." In all of these outcries there is a cast of elitism: that what was a special place, a powerful experience, for a singular soul at a singular time, was the right experience; and all else is somehow something less.

Besides, the articulation of the concept is wrong. Wilderness, which is nature unchanged by the hand of man, is not generally adversely affected by small groups of softly-stepping people passing quickly through, whether they carry tents, paddles, Gore-Tex or computers and phones. As long as they leave only footprints and kill only time, the wilderness pretty much remains as such. What does change is the notion of the "wilderness experience." In my mind, the only absolute wilderness experience is one in which you cut the tether and surrender yourself to the elements...there is no nexus to the world of humans and machines; you're as raw as a feral dog. As such, if I went naked into just beyond my backyard, into a grove of old growth, my wilderness experience would be more genuine than anyone standing on the roof of Everest, wrapped in layers of manufactured apparel and connected to the world through technology. If you accept this notion, then the wilderness experience becomes one of degree. Is it more or less so if you use the gear and clothing available in 1953? Is it less so if you carry a radio for emergencies, or a cell phone? What if you have Internet access, but you don't read your e-mail?

In fact, the Internet and mobile communications are not the death of wilderness. They may be its savior.

With its power to break the tyranny of geography, to allow people anywhere in the world to virtually join expeditions to wild places through the portals of their computer screens, and its capacity for information exchange and communications, the Internet can be a more effective tool than anything yet devised to preserve the wilderness. The ledger is long of wilderness areas gone down because there wasn't a constituency to do battle. The rainforests of northern Sumatra, where I thrashed in the early 1980s, and where orangutans once ruled, is now a tropical desert due to timber poachers. I made the first-descent of the Grand Canyon of the Euphrates River in Turkey in the late 1970s—an utterly breathtaking corridor filled with ancient castles and ruins—but nobody followed in my wake, and within a decade it was buried beneath a dam-created lake. Arizona's and Utah's Glen Canyon, also entombed beneath an artificial lake, is the poster child. A basic problem is that wilderness areas are hard to get to, and the numbers who see them, experience them, fall in love with them, are too often too small to make a difference. That's where the internet and mobile communications can be instruments of awareness, appreciation and activism that no oversized nature book ever could.

For the first time we can showcase the beauty and magic of a wild place to a global audience, and millions can participate in a journey through it, without ever breaking a branch or stepping on cryptobiotic soil. To a degree, *National Geographic* has done this for over a century in the pages of its august journal; and Discovery and others have done this on television and video. But those were passive receiver experiences, where a publisher, editor or producer added his or her own vision to the primary experience, passing it along to a quiescent audience. Now, for the first time, a worldwide audience can receive the data unfiltered from the primary reporter, in all its raw and brutal honesty. And members of that same audience can become players, become active on some levels, participating in the experience by asking questions, suggesting ideas, and sharing information.

The Internet, and with it mobile communications, are the most powerful intercommunications tools yet, ones that tear down the media power towers. They erase the information filters of middlemen, and allow anyone to jump into the thick of things and asseverate a voice and opinion. Those who joined, through the web, my 1996 expedition down the Tekeze "experienced" canyons grander than the Grand, saw and heard baboons, monkeys and riverside flutes, and rode along as we ran rapids and were chased by crocodiles. And, they learned that a scheme existed to dam this extraordinary wilderness. I'm convinced that when the time comes for a call to action to stop the drowning of the Tekeze, the patronage for preservation will be that much greater for the Web. A dozen years ago we lost a fight to save Chile's crown jewel of a wild river, the Bio-Bio, from the concrete slug of a private big dam; but then only a few thousand had ever seen the river. Now more people than visit Yosemite in August, regardless of wallet size, physical abilities, age or weight, can be introduced to a faraway wilderness in a more immediate way, and that means that many more who can fall in love with a wild place, grasp its issues, and perhaps lend a hand when it needs many. In this there is merit in the new digital nomadism.

But the downside remains that this new nomadism isolates cliques, and has widespread sociologic ill effects. A century ago some saw the car merely as a faster camel, yet it led to entirely new cities, with suburbs and sprawl, to new retail cultures (megastores, drive-throughs), new dependencies (oil) and new health threats (sloth, obesity). By the same token, wireless technology is surely not just an easier-to-use phone.

Digital nomadism will liberate ever more knowledge, but the old tyranny of place could become a new tyranny of time, as nomads who are "always on" all too often end up—mentally—anywhere but here (wherever here may be). There is a fountain in the Redmond Town Center close to where I used to work, and I would sometimes take Walker there to play. On weekends it was as crowded as The Grand Socco here in Morocco. It was a font of e-mailers and cell phoners, and we never, in nine years, made a connection with a stranger.

There are many upsides to digital nomadism, such as wilderness preservation, and political transparencies. The same tools that isolate can also improve the world: witness the spectacular coverage of the planet by camera phones. They turn practically everybody into a potential human rights activist, ready to take pictures or video of injustice, just as presence in a Kasbah, with many people in each room, kept behavior in check. But the same tools have a dark side, turning everybody into a fully equipped paparazzo. As in the desert, so in the city: nomadism promises the heaven of new freedom, but it also threatens the hell of constant surveillance by the tribe.

22. MEANING IN NOTHINGNESS

"The eternal aspects of mankind are always present. There is a purity that belongs to an older age, and everywhere there is a direct communication with the past; in family relationships, in local dress, in the prevalent code of manners. Morocco is and has always been a deeply mystical land."

–Lisa Lovatt-Smith, *Moroccan Interiors*, 1995

From Tangier we head out among long drops of rain to make the two-and-a-half hour drive to Rabat, the capital, so anointed by the French, on the Atlantic coast. Morocco's second-largest city is a salty seaside town where bronze canons stand in unroused retirement. Rabat's origins are in the 8th century BC when people settled in nearby Chellah. When the Roman Empire crumbled, Berbers turned the Kasbah here into a ribat (fortress-monastery). As the Berber Saint Augustine said, "The world is a book, and those who do not travel read only a page." There are a lot of chapters here.

In the 17th century, Andalusian Moors fleeing the Spanish Inquisition built a new city south of the Kasbah which they called Bou Regreg.

Meanwhile, sister city Salé, on the east side of the river, had become notorious. Andalusian refugees teamed up with Berber inhabitants and international undesirables, and turned to piracy on the high seas.

These corsairs (sea raiders) were the notorious "Salle Rovers," and for more than 300 years they terrorized shipping and coastal communities in the Atlantic and Mediterranean. Men, women and children from as far away as Cornwall in southern England were nabbed at sea and from their homes, streets and fields to suffer lives of deprivation and hard labor. Robinson Crusoe was a fictional captive of a "Turkish rover of Sallee."

Here I again meet up with Chakib, now natty in his suit, and ask if he can arrange a couple of high-level meetings, and in short order he does.

The colors are seeping back into the world as Chakib meets me in front of the Hilton hotel. We drive through the city, which is as quiet now as it is busy as sunset; the only sign of life is the smoke rising solemnly from the bakeries. We stop for coffee, bitter and thick, and a croissant. Then, a short time later I find myself in the vast office of Abdelhamid Addou, the CEO of the Moroccan Tourist Office, an important post as Tourism is Morocco's top source of hard currency. He offers tea, and asks me to sit by a large low coffee table and ask any questions.

"What is different about Morocco?" I begin.

"Well, we have a deep and dynamic culture, yet at the same time a tradition of openness and tolerance. Like America, we are a melting pot. Yet even though we are a Muslim country, people of all religions live and thrive here. The mix is unique. And, we have a genuine 'Living Culture.' Unlike most other places, people here are still living, by choice, the way they did 800 years ago…they live in the monuments, in the Kasbahs, in nomadic tents. They make the same arts and crafts. There is a kind of mystical link to the past.

"And I would add that we are a crossroads and a mosaic. We are the crossroads between Europe and Africa; a crossroads between religions and cultures. And we are a mosaic of weather and geography. Where else can you ski in the morning, drive two hours and have tea in the desert, and then drive two more hours and swim in the ocean?"

"So, what is the spirit of the Kasbah?" I feel like an infant wrestling with a king-sized mattress.

"The Kasbah is a kind of crossroads as well. It was built first as a castle to protect families from invaders, but when the families felt secure, it became a way station for nomads, travelers bringing new ideas, architectures and food. It was a place to share experiences. And tolerance was the mortar that held it all together. Now the Kasbah represents the personality and soul of all of Morocco. It is inviting guests for tea, the beginning of hospitality. It is authenticity, openness, safety and tolerance. As we did in the Kasbahs hundreds of years ago, we welcome visitors...they are invited into our homes and treated like princes...we know that if people understand each other, then there is peace. We have everything to share, and nothing to hide. Our doors are open."

23. NO INTENT ON ARRIVING

"Kings rule men, wise men rule kings."
–Abu el-Aswad, 681 AD

Afterwards Chakib wheels me to the Royal Palace, and after clearing a gauntlet of security checks, I am ushered to the dark paneled offices of Andre Azoulay, the Essaouira-born Sephardic Jew and former Paris-based investment banker who 20 years ago accepted an offer to be a counselor to the king. He invites me into his book-lined office, and gives me a lengthy handshake. Even though he has served two kings, and is past retirement age, he is alert, like a greyhound in the starting trap. We sit, and share some tea, and he tells me he wasn't born yesterday.

"I like to say I am 3000 years old. Most people don't know that Judaism came to Morocco more than 1000 years before Islam; 600 years before Jesus Christ. We have always seen ourselves as a world center."

He speaks with the assurance of stature, but with none of its arrogance.

"And the reason is that we feel comfortable and strong ourselves. It gives us an ideology that welcomes others. It's not a risky proposition for us. In some ways you don't need a passport here. The passport is art and music."

Andre's love of art and music traces to his childhood in Essaouira. He remembers walking the streets and hearing music that had no distinction between Jew and Muslim. And he remembers Orson Welles.

Orson Welles had planned to shoot the film of his version of *Othello* in Venice, but he discovered he didn't have the budget. So, he found Essaouira as a cheaper, and in many ways, more colorful alternative. Local Jewish women made the armor for the costumes from sardine cans, saving the production a lot of clams.

Seeking extras, Welles hired many of the local school children, including Andre Azoulay, and the director paid them with a little bread and chocolate every day for two months.

But the impressionable and important moment was when the great film-maker received the Grand Prix at Cannes for the film in 1952. Morocco at that time was under the French mandate. Welles, however, decided to give the Palme D'Or to Morocco as a nation, and he asked the orchestra to play the Moroccan national anthem. "All the Moroccans alive at that moment will never forget it. Orson Welles gave us our dignity four years before we got it officially with independence."

Essaouira has been a personal passion for Azoulay ever since, and he is chief architect of the town's revival and rising status as a world music and festival center. "You can create wealth through art and culture, and I have helped make that happen in my home town. When I first became an advisor to the King there were six hotels in Essaouira…now there are 229, thanks to the music and the festivals that have become world famous. We'll sometimes have as many as half a million festival goers in a city of 80,000."

Azoulay settles back in his chair, and rounds his shoulders as he continues.

"In a certain way we are lucky in Morocco to not have oil. Culture is our oil. We base everything on our human resources. Civilization has great value…it means something to us. We make ourselves committed to fight for universal values and freedom, and we are proud of from where we are coming. Culture here is more important than ideology, more important than economic theory. There are alternatives to hatred and disrespect, including mutual understanding and working together."

Azoulay has taken the lessons of Essaouira and applied them to the world stage. "My life goal is to help effect the reconciliation of the Jews and Arabs in the Middle East, and I have helped in several key negotiations between the Israelis and the Palestinians. In Morocco we have seen no deportations, no Nazism, no concentration camps and no Inquisition whatsoever. Rather, we have seen Jews and Muslims living together and respecting each other. We harbored thousands of Jews during the war, and when the Vichy government asked the King for support, he said we don't have Jews or Arabs here…we have Moroccans. And he said that if the Nazis demanded that Jews in Morocco wear the yellow star, then he would be the first to wear it.

"We have seen a relationship develop that was globally positive," he explains. "We want to tell the world that something other than just war and bloodshed is possible in Arab-Jewish relations. Our examples can be found among our fellow Moroccans. Among the Arabs of Morocco, many share the goals of identity and dialogue. They consider that what they have experienced with their fellow Moroccan Jews is part of the national heritage, and therefore must be protected.

"Just open the history book. When America still didn't exist, when European countries were breaking stones to survive, we were sending all over the world mathematicians, philosophers, musicians, writers. We were always travelers. Our openness and outward looking perspective is very, very deeply rooted. We are a continuation of what we started hundreds of years ago. It is not a gadget. It is our way to protect history, identity, and local values. It is powerful and critical. We embrace the modern world; we enter it with excitement, but always without losing our roots, our soul and our spirit.

"Morocco has been and will be a champion of the universal dimension of humanity.

"I am fortunate to belong to a very exclusive club, so selective and snobbish I am the only member—a Jewish advisor to an Arab King. But that has helped me negotiate…and I will not give up."

Chakib wants to show off his town, so from the palace we head over to the Hassan Mosque, the pink-stoned 140-foot-high watchtower built by Sultan Yacoub al-Mansour at the close of the 12th century, and Rabat's major landmark. Though never finished, it may have been the largest mosque in the world, until an earthquake in 1775 destroyed most of the original tower and columns.

It is adjacent to the white-sided, green-roofed mausoleum of Mohammed V, the Moroccan king who negotiated the country's independence from France in 1956, and who died in 1961. As such the whole compound is walled and guarded by Royal sentinels looking spiffy in blood-red uniforms, white caps and belts, green fez caps and rifles at arm's length. The low sun beating down on the compound seems to strengthen these soldiers, making them taller and swarthier.

Just outside the massive Bab er Rouah, Gate of the Wind, are *nakkachat*, women with syringes full of henna mixed with water and lemon juice, ready to pipe a design onto the hands of the willing tourist, as if decorating a cake. I watch as one visitor from Los Angeles, the actress Lourdes Uribe, sits and is festooned with inky flowers and patterns, reflected in her large secret agent sunglasses.

Next we head over to the ruins of Chellah, passing the high-walled American embassy along the way. That which remains, remains. Chellah was the first place to be settled along the Bou Regreg River in the third century BC. Archeologists think it probable that Phoenicians and Carthaginians inhabited the banks. The Romans took over in 40 AD and turned it into Sala Colonia. It was one of the last outposts to sever ties with the empire. Around 250 AD it came under the control of Berber rulers.

Chellah was abandoned in 1154, but then later used by the Almohad dynasty as a necropolis, and among those buried was Abou el Hassan, known as the Black Sultan because his mother was Ethiopian—a relative of the guide I had met in Addis Ababa some years before. In the middle of the 14th century Hassan had constructed a mosque, a Zawiya, and a grand main gate here. The massive earthquake in the 18th century tumbled much that stood here as well.

Muslims believe that Paradise is a garden, and today Chellah is a garden sanctuary of hibiscus, figs and dragon trees, dominated by a blizzard of cattle egrets and clacking storks who have built nests on weathered pillars and broken tops of columns that look like minarets on top of minarets. Storks in Moroccan culture are a sign of good fortune. As are feral cats and eels, who also have presence. There is a little dark ablutions pool where women feed boiled eggs to gray eels for good luck, and to aid in childbirth. I stoop to pet a tortoiseshell-patterned kitten with a snowy breast and cabochon eyes, and count my blessings.

Then Chakib instructs Mohammed to drive us to the storybook Kasbah des Oudaias, where each building resembles a breaking wave - painted brilliant blue and dazzling white higher up. The Kasbah stands as it has for centuries, aloof atop the cliffs overlooking the Atlantic and the Bou Regreg River, keeping watch over the mouth of the river, the inland plain and the little boats ferrying people to Salé, Rabat's gleaming white sister city on the right bank of the river. Gauzy light, particular to the North African Atlantic coast, warms the air gently, but effectively. Matisse, who spent two winters in Morocco, claimed to have found paradise, and learned to reconcile abstraction and decoration with realism, and his paintings became tender, fluid—"fire," as one critic said, "filtered though water," all as cool "as a freshly opened almond."

NO INTENT ON ARRIVING

The bones of this Kasbah practically shiver with its pirate past. The corsairs were successful because the crews were made up of a whirlpool of international talent, just another example of Morocco's melting pot. One of the techniques employed here was to lure Spanish galleons close to shore in pursuit of pirate ships, only to be caught fast on the barely submerged sandbar. Then the low-keeled pirate vessels breezed a few hundred yards upriver to safety while the cannons of the Kasbah loosed their firepower on the stranded ships.

Down narrow, labyrinthine streets we step to Café des Oudaias, a superbly sited terrace tearoom with a view of the river and Salé. We take a seat at a bright blue table, under a shady trellis, and peruse the menu. Though coffee is readily available, the preference is sweet mint tea, and pastries such as coconut macaroons, cornes de gazelle (horn-shaped cakes) filled with almond paste, or "cigares," dripping with honey in the shape of a finger or a triangle. But all the sweetness is overwhelmed by the sour smell of the sea, and the knowledge that it's time to move on, as a white house awaits us.

24. AS TIME GOES BY

"Il faut être absolument moderne." (We have to be absolutely modern).
– Arthur Rimbaud, *A Season in Hell*, 1873

We make the hour drive to the conurbations of Casablanca, which for much of the world is more a film than a place. *Casablanca*, the movie, was made in 1942 against the backdrop of the Second World War, with the remnants of French colonialism still very much in evidence throughout North Africa.

Today, Casablanca, the city, is a quantum center of commerce, an expanse of white colonial architecture and imposing Moorish buildings; a seething metropolis of glass towers and grand buildings. Casablanca, meaning "White House," is a city of period styles. The cupolas, towers, columns and oriels whirl with Art Deco elements, an artistry that inspired the likes of Edith Piaf, Albert Camus and Saint-Exupery.

We make our way down a palm-lined boulevard to stop at the grandest of buildings, the second biggest mosque in the world (after the al-Haram mosque in Mecca) and largest in Africa, the Hassan II Mosque, built for the 60th birthday of former Moroccan King Hassan II. Its glittering gold, pink, bone and green façade dominates the skyline, seeming to float in the air; part of it actually hangs over the Atlantic Ocean. Like so much of Morocco, even the religious architecture is a fusion of form, styles, concepts and technologies, and this piece, designed by a Frenchman, incorporates elements from all over the world. Built between 1987 and 1993, it is said to have cost $750 million, and is breathtaking in terms of its opulent decoration and scale—the minaret is nearly 50 stories high, and features a blue laser beam that shoots toward Mecca, as the mosque is meant to be a "lighthouse for Islam." The prayer hall can hold 25,000 worshippers (another 80,000 can fit on the outside esplanades), and I'm told that St. Paul's Cathedral could fit inside. It is also the only working mosque in Morocco that can be entered by non-Muslims. I take off my shoes, and pad through the enormous titanium doors and across the centrally heated cream-colored marble floor. Above, some 77 chandeliers cast an ethereal, blue light. The ablution hall sprouts 42 fountains. There are doors everywhere, with a range in size equal to those Alice wandered through in Wonderland. It's all too intoxicating.

It's time for a drink. I need a gin joint.

In the film *Casablanca*, there's a wry exchange between Humphrey Bogart's character, Rick Blaine, and Capt. Renault, played by Claude Raines, in which Renault asks Rick what "in heaven's name" brought him to Casablanca in the first place.

"My health," Rick knocks back. "I came to Casablanca for the waters."

"The waters?" Renault replies. "What waters? We're in the desert."

"I was misinformed."

In truth, the deep sea port of Casablanca lies at the end of a fertile agricultural plain; it's not the desert. But there are so many myths associated with the film, the city and the country.

So, I am shocked, shocked to find there actually is a Rick's Café in Casablanca. At the northern end of the walls of the Ancienne Medina, along the waterfront Boulevard Sour Jdid (Arabic for "new walls"), there is an arched doorway up a set of stairs. Stepping through it is like tumbling through time, back to 1942, in the midst of a world war. The period décor, architecture and lighting are all so familiar. There is an Arabesque windowed cupola, filled with white archways and patios. There are white-linened tables topped with beaded lamps. Black rattan chairs. Moucharabieh screens, behind which conspiracies are plotted. Waiters with crisp white shirts and tasseled red fezes. There are palm trees, a winding staircase with iron balustrades, a long green marbled bar, a replica of the film's. But there is one stark difference…everything is in color!

I take a seat, and order caviar (it is the only food seen in the movie), and say, "Waiter, a bottle of Veuve Clicquot 1926, a very good wine," which of course is what Captain Renault ordered for Major Strasser's table. They seem to be out, so instead he brings me Dom Perignon, which I sip from a flute and take in the view. It is like a modern Kasbah, in that it seems a safe haven, a touchstone, a gathering place for cultures and ideas…among the unusual suspects I hear a babble of languages, and universal laughter, and the common clink of glasses. Dominating the central courtyard is a beautiful piano, an authentic Pleyel from the 30s, and after a few minutes out walks the tuxedoed player, Issam Chabaa. Who could resist?

"Play it again, Issam," I say, along with hundreds before me. And he launches into a fluid rendition of "As Time Goes By." Just like so many myths about Morocco, the famous line, "Play it again, Sam," was never delivered in the movie, just like there was no Rick's Café Americain in Casablanca, which for years was a surprise to many American visitors. Until now.

And the role of Rick, today, is played by Kathy Kriger.

Kathy hails from a small town outside of Portland, Oregon, and worked around the world, first as owner of a travel agency (she used to book my Sobek trips), and then as a diplomat. She had no idea she would end up in Casablanca, but in 1993 she visited an Australian psychic, Manfred, who predicted she would settle in a warm place. His words: "I see palm trees, I see water."

In 1998 she was dispatched to Morocco as a US diplomat, where one of her first assignments was to oversee Hillary Clinton's visit to Marrakech. But after the events of September 11, 2001, Kathy was dismayed at how much of the West misperceived Morocco, and how the world beyond became more xenophobic. Cruise ships docked here, and passengers refused to get off. She decided to see if she might help in some small way, and decided to leave the cocoon of the diplomatic corps and take the entrepreneurial risk and "re-establish" the most famous gin-joint ever, Rick's Café.

I ask Kathy if she might chat for a few minutes, and she invites me upstairs to a room where an endless loop of the eponymous film plays against one wall, always "Mit Out Sound." Still, there is period music piped in, and she calls for her staff to turn it down, and pulls up a wicker chair. I begin by asking why the movie, which is often cited as the greatest film of all time, is so ever popular.

"Well, it's a love story, but it's also a story of loyalty, of difficult decisions, and of standing up for what's right....it evokes the values of destiny and dignity....these are international values, and they resonate here. And there is a natural nostalgia for times gone by.

"Was it hard for a woman to create and take on such an enterprise?" I ask.

"Destiny is mentioned a lot in the film, and this was my destiny. There were challenges, as with any business start-up, but Morocco is an amazingly supportive place. I had no issues as a woman in an Arab country with business ambitions. People here are accepted for who they are. And respected. It doesn't matter gender or religion or where you come from. Taking care of others is a core tenet, as it has been for hundreds of years."

Looking around the room I see several movie posters featuring Humphrey Bogart, and have to ask:

"Has a Bogie look-alike come in?

"No, but we did have a dead ringer for Peter Lorre as Ugarte in the film. And Monika Henreid, the daughter of actor Paul Henreid who played Victor Lazlo in the film, has been here three times, once to celebrate her birthday. And there are lots of Germans...they love the film."

"It's crowded downstairs. It seems the concept is successful."

"Well, yes, there are over six decades of pent-up desire for a real Rick's, and now, like in the film, we are in turbulent times. This is a little refuge. This is Morocco writ small. It is a place that welcomes anyone; it is open to anyone. It is a place to meet and exchange drinks, good food, conversation and ideas. It is, in a way, a modern Kasbah. And the best part is, when I look out the window I see palm trees, I see water."

25. TIME WOUNDS ALL HEELS

"I was born for the storm, and a calm does not suit me."
– Andrew Jackson, 1813

It is now the start of summer, and my son Walker, now 13, is out of school and wants to join me in Morocco. I'm eager to continue our explorations, and propose another rash undertaking....that we make a trek to the Riff Mountains, the Mediterranean coastal range where the grass is greener, so they say. Not many tourists yet venture here. Yet it has one of the highest mountains in North Africa, Jbel Tidiquin, 8031 feet above the sea, and I would love to climb it.

We team up with a wonderful driver, Ahmed El Abdi, who takes us first to Tangier for the night, where we are given the room, we are told, used by Bernardo Bertolucci when he filmed his version of Paul Bowles' novel *The Sheltering Sky*. It has a dark-wood chair inlaid with fragments of mother-of-pearl that is exquisitely uncomfortable. Adjacent is a fine bureau with tooled cabriole legs, and when I open one of the miniature drawers there is a scrap of crumpled paper with illegible scrawling. I wonder if this might be some script notes from the mind of a genius filmmaker.

It reminds me of a moment some years ago when I stayed at Francis Ford Coppola's Blancaneaux Lodge in the glazed hills of Belize. It was during the off-season, and the eco-resort was near empty, so the manager offered that I stay in Francis's private bungalow. I looked around his room and saw portraits of his extended family, including Nicholas Cage and Sofia Coppola; piles of scripts, and notes scribbled on scraps of paper. This was a creative retreat for the director, and he came here to find inspiration, the manager said brightly. I happened to be carrying a few of the books I had authored, so I scattered them around the room, and put some in the dresser drawers, hoping Francis might find something he liked and give me a call. I'm still waiting.

So, here, too, I have a couple of my books, and I slip one into the bureau drawer. You never know.

The day following we make the five hour drive from Tangier to the village of Chefchaouen (which means "look at the peaks"). Along the way we stop and Walker enjoys a number of "firsts," his first camel ride, his first cup of coffee, and his first "monkey shower," when a road-side handler places the primate on Walker's shoulder for a photo op. One "first" he refuses is a hookah suck. At the back of a roadside café curved like the shell of a snail, men are drawing conspiratorially on giant hubble-bubble pipes, and so I order up one with two hoses. When it arrives I show him how it works, and the water gurgles, as a cloud of smoke curls the air. But Walker declines the cool smoke, and orders a Coke instead.

We pass cork forest and olive groves, soaring brick minarets trimmed with white, flocks of black goats and off-white sheep, and most provocative to Walker's eye, shepherdesses in scarlet hats, white tops, boots and bright red knickerbocker leggings.

The sun is burning low and coppery when we pass through the Bab el-Majorrol gate into Chefchaouen, which happens to be a sister city of Issaquah, Washington, where I enjoyed many a hike when I lived in adjacent Redmond, and the two towns, I must say, would seem to have little in common. Up a steep, steep hill we grind, the engine sounding like a spoon caught in a disposal. We pull into the Atlas Riad Chaouen, nestled in a saddle beneath the stark limestone rock face of Ain Tissemlal (3280') and Jebel el Kelaa (4206'), known together as Ech-Chaoua (the horns). Though in the shadow of these peaks, the hotel at the same time hangs high above the village, like the lair of a Doctor Seuss character. We drop our bags in the room, which is filled with the swish of the wind from the eucalyptus trees outside the single window. We pull back the curtains and are dazzled by a flood of canary yellow light. But when our eyes adjust we gape at a view of medieval houses whitened with a bluish lime—the walls shine in the sun like a glacier.

Walker is restless, and wants to stretch legs, so we decide to take a short hike to the ruins of a 250-year-old Portuguese mosque on a slope across the main river valley. It's a hot hike, but it feels cooler for the long view from the crumbling tower across the river to the medina. Try to imagine the coolest, most mouth-wateringly liquid blue you've ever wanted to drink or dive into on a hot day: the homes in Chefchaouen are painted that color.

On the way back to the hotel we dip down into the little canyon of the Oued Laou, its banks ablaze with bright pink oleander, and its shallows filled with women washing and children splashing. After crossing a small bridge we thread through the eastern gate of the medina, Bab el-Ansar, into the compact, cobalt blue-washed world via its steep and maze-like walkways.

Even the stairs are dyed soft blue or cream. It makes the ice cream for sale from little carts irresistible, and we indulge in some soupy blue scoops on cones. Then we wander the worn cobbled alleyways, some so narrow Walker's long outstretched arms can touch both walls. We pass beneath tiny balconies, past little shops selling woven blankets, cedar wood antiques, necklaces of silver and red coral, and fennec furs. The tea houses are crowded but breezy with chat and brews. No cell phones here; just a cool, serene atmosphere. Blue is the overriding color; there is no seam between building and sky…it's like walking along the bottom of a resort pool.

Originally a fortress town, Chefchaouen was founded in 1471 to halt the advance of the Iberians after their capture of Ceuta to the north (still a Spanish protectorate), and served as a religious sanctuary for Muslims and Jews absquatulating from Granada. A series of dynasties ruled the area, long a center for Sufi mysticism, and the 'zouia' brotherhoods still practice their rites and traditions today. Access for Christians, however, was only gained in 1920, when Spanish troops occupied northern Morocco. Before then, the tourist brochure trumpets, only three Westerners had ever visited this secret base. The invading Spanish found a time capsule of their own culture. They also heard a form of 10th-century Catalan, a language brought by the Andalucían Jews, which had died out on the Iberian Peninsula four centuries before. They also found Granada leatherwork, pottery and other crafts long extinct in their native country.

Now, Hispano-Moorish influence is apparent everywhere: in the clematis-covered archways that span the streets, in the narrow barred windows, and in the studded doorways that open onto sun-drenched patios. However, the singularly most stunning elements are the blue-painted buildings, soaked in different shades of turquoise and azure, producing a semi-mirage effect. The blue wash only came about in the 1930s, when Jewish refugees finally decided to paint over the previously Muslim-green window frames and doors.

Thirsty, we agree to sit and sip glasses of mint tea at one of the shops, one cluttered with treasure, and weighed down by a mountain of bargains. There are ancient Berber chests, silver teapots, ebony footstools, and weapons once used by warring tribes. Walker's eyes brighten, and he soon finds himself tangled in the art of negotiating. He has the habit of rationing his conversation, which works to his advantage, as when his silences are long, the salesman breaks the quiet by punching his pocket calculator and lowering his price. Walker ends up buying an antique pistol for $30….the opening price was $3000, so he feels pretty trick about the deal, even though the salesman claims the firearm is older than gunpowder. I submit to a couple of *kelims*, the short rugs originally made to cushion the knees of the devout when they prayed towards Mecca, but now lining the walls and hallways of the infidels in the west. With our bootie in hand we head back up the hill, beads of sweat popping off our brows like insects. We pass a line of women in red and white striped overskirts and large conical straw hats with woolen bobbles, and they seem cool as cucumbers despite the heat. We beat it back to the hotel, which though modest in most regards, is generous in its air conditioning, and we sit back and enjoy the arctic air.

Almost nobody speaks English here—Arabic and Spanish are the lingua francas—which is in a way refreshing, and it prompts Walker and me to talk in ways we don't when in restaurants back home. We point to items on the menu, and the waiter hovers like a black and white butterfly, nods, and then flits away. When he returns he serves us in a way that seems almost protective, as though there is a religious dimension to the hospitality, to the supper and succor for strangers.

After dinner I importune the front desk manager, who does speak a crumb of English, if he can help us find a guide to take us climbing tomorrow. "Ah, you want to go up our mountain…here we call it Mount Baldy" he informs, and Walker pulls off my hat and chuckles that it is the appropriate mountain for me.

"Yes. Can you find us a good guide?"

"Of course; the best. Be here in the lobby at 10:00 am.

"Isn't that a bit late? Its summer…it gets hot. Shouldn't we start quite early to avoid the midday heat while hiking?

"No, no…you will be fine. Besides my guide doesn't start before 10:00."

26. ONCE AN EXPERIMENT, TWICE A PERVERSION

"I learnt the satisfaction which comes from hardship and the pleasure which springs from abstinence,"
– Wilfred Thesiger, *Arabian Sands*, 1959

The sky lightens slowly the next morning, and time seems to pour like treacle as we linger through breakfast. At last, about 10:30 Moroccan Time, Anass Hazim, 27, saunters into the lobby and extends his hand. His skin is parched and rough and feels like the hand of a reptile. He tells us he has been a guide for seven years, and has climbed Mount Baldy many times—we have nothing to worry about. It should take a nice and easy three hours for the whole enterprise. But I am a little leery of his leather leisure shoes, even if it is but a stroll. I ask about water, and he says, not to worry, we won't need any. But that doesn't feel right, so I quickly buy four plastic bottles of Sidi Ali water from the restaurant and stuff them into my pack. He piles us into a car, and we drive through twenty shades of moonscape into the Parc National de Talassemtane, to a settlement called Akchour.

We park at the foot of a low dam on the river Kelaa. The surrounding mountains are all burnt umber and dusty taupe, scarred with horizontal serrations, jutting up in every direction. Here we shoulder our packs, and start walking up the side of the river, past oleander bushes, through stands of Holm oak and feathery pines, and alongside steep cliffs. It's arduous and hot, following the contours of the gorge, so hot it sends chills down my arms. Walker and I each swallow a bottle of water in the first hour. I'm a little surprised to note that Anass doesn't wear sunglasses or a hat, and to see that he smokes constantly, but perhaps that is the norm in Morocco. Our guide in the Atlas, Rachid, did as well. But there is something about Anass that doesn't quite seem guide-like. His eyes are not far-reaching as are the eyes of most of the wilderness guides I have known. He seems to focus more on the surface of the present.

About noon we come to a natural stone arch that crosses the river, the Pont de Dieu or "God's Window," and here Walker announces he doesn't want to go any farther. He wants to wait here in the shade by the bridge. "It's too hot, Dad." I'm okay with that, and since it must only be a short walk from here to the top, I figure we will be up and back in an hour. But Anass doesn't want to go any farther either.

"Why not?" I ask. "You're the professional mountain guide."

He draws his face into hundreds of little wrinkles, not in a squint, but as if his face is drawing inward to escape a truth.

"I have not guided beyond here before....only to the bridge."

"What?"

"Tourists don't go past here."

"Well, I am...you have to come with me...you're the guide."

So, I leave a bottle of water with Walker, and tuck the last one in my fanny pack for easy access, and Anass and I start the sheer climb. It is a faint trail, zigzagging through the cedars and brush, and after a few minutes I can look up and see what looks like the summit. But suddenly Anass stops.

"We must turn around."

"I don't understand. Why? We can see the top."

"No, that is not the top…there are four more peaks beyond that to the summit, and you have to go up and down steep valleys. It will take three days." He gives me a glaze like the gleam off a knife.

"But you said three hours."

"It is too dangerous to continue. It is a technical climb."

"What do you mean? We're on a path…let's keep going."

I turn and start to hike and Anass follows me grudgingly. I stop after a few minutes, and take a draw on the water bottle, and offer some to Anass…his brow is glistening with sweat as he takes a long drink, and then announces he is turning back.

"You can't turn back…you are my guide."

He clearly isn't gripped with this idea.

"You must turn back with me…there are wild Barbary apes near the top…they will attack you. I know this."

This gives me pause…the image of fending off a troop of wild macaques, alone on a hot mountain, is not favorable. But I catch myself…this can't be true.

"I'm going on Anass even without you."

He screws up his face until his eyes are no more than slits.

"You should not. If I get into trouble that is okay; but if you get into trouble, it is a big problem for me."

"I'm sorry Anass….you go check on Walker. I'll hike to the top, and be back soon."

He gives me a gimlet glare, then turns on his heel and heads down the hill.

I realize now how brutal the sun is…it is midday, and there is no shade as I continue. But I am convinced it is but a short ways to the summit, and then I can turn back and reunite with Walker and the river.

But as I get closer to the top it seems to roll away, as though on wheels. And then the trail careens off to the side…I follow it, and it takes me over a shoulder that reveals another peak higher than what I had been watching. But it is not so far, so I continue. And I take judicious sips from my water bottle.

After another 30 minutes of hiking I breach another pass, and see there is still another higher peak. I weigh the options, wipe my brow, and decide it's better to continue…it can't be that much farther.

But it is…I struggle up a steep section, and rise to another false summit, and stare at a new, higher summit, but this one is across a wide and deep valley. It does look as though it might take days to traverse this route. Anass was right. But the good news, I tell myself, is there are no Barbary Apes in sight.

So, I take a long draw from my plastic bottle, and begin the return hike, now most certainly not overburdened with an abundance of water. Along the way I notice something I had missed coming up….discarded clothing. There is a pair of blue socks; a while later, a sweater. And then at a sharp bend in the path, a pair of trousers. What happened here, I wonder, that people abandoned their clothes on this trail?

It is getting hotter. The heat is rippling, like just out of a kiln. I stop every hundred yards or so and try to rest in the scant shelter of a scrawny cedar. I pull a branch from the tree—it smells like soap— and turn it into a hiking stick. I take the last few sips of water.

Then I start to feel the onset of heat exhaustion: dizziness, muscle weakness and nausea. My throat is dry; my lips cracked. The heat bites at the corners of my eyes. I feel a sweat fever coming on, though I feel no sweat. In a landscape as this one can sweat four gallons a day without realizing it. The sweat evaporates too quickly to be noticed.

I know what happens next....the throat constricts, the body temperature soars. Disorientation, hallucinations, gagging and liver failure follow, and then coma and death. On the upside, I could qualify for a Darwin Award.

The sky is anything but sheltering here, but Paul Bowles would appreciate this setting, I believe. He derived his most famous title from a popular World War I tune, "Down Among the Sheltering Palms." Because in the Sahara there is only the sky, Bowles omitted the palms, leaving the fine fabric of the sky. Bowles presented the new conditions of modernity, ground rules for the infidel: the sky is the thin membrane between life and death, the traveler's final frontier, and the last obstacle to repose.

I stop and sit on a lozenge of stone for a spell, and watch as a high-tufted Houbara bustard lands on a crag and struts about.

I envy the bird. I want to fly. No, I want to rest, and lower my head into my lap. I can feel my body wilt and weaken. I fight for clarity in the mayhem of my mind. I curl into a little ball with my arms wrapped tightly around my knees and become a pebble on this path. I am, at this place, at this time, unessential to the world. But then I shake my head vigorously, and pull myself up leaning on my stick. I know I have to continue. I'm out of water, and there are no other people on this trail in the summer heat of the Riff. I pull out my cell phone, but there is no service.

So, downwards I stagger, my legs making long steps as if of their own accord. Had I jockeyed my horse into a flaming barn, I wonder? The faint path seems to divide into three, and I take the left one, as I lean that way. But after a time it peters out, and I am thrashing through sharp scrub. I'm lost. This is not the Lost of the Fès medina, or of Burgundy, or the Atlas, or even Ethiopia. This is a lost that could have serious consequences in short order. I turn around and scrape back up the hill to the tracings of the path, and take the middle way.

After a spell I think I am beginning to hallucinate. I see a pond, and walk towards it, but it wavers away. I think I see a woman hiker and yell to her, but as I get closer I see she has the feet of a goat. She must be Aisha Qandisha, the Moroccan siren who lures people to their doom, causes uncontrollable ecstasy and ultimately destructive obsession. But as I warily move towards her she turns into a tree. I am accompanied only by myself. Having worked as a guide in the Grand Canyon, I know the dangers of heat exhaustion, and I recognize that I am sliding into a dodgy state. But what is the choice?

What was I thinking taking this trek alone in the midday sun? I am not Thesiger and his Bedouin, but a lesser mortal who has spent most of my adventuring on water. Now I am without my favored element, and suffering for it.

It is said that a Sufi dervish wanders the earth because the action of walking dissolves the attachments of the world, and that his aim is to become a "dead man walking," a man whose feet are rooted on the ground but whose spirit is already in Heaven. I wonder if I am at this moment a dead man walking, though I can barely take a step, so perhaps it is a dead man stumbling.

At last I see the Kelaa canyon rim, I think...it wobbles rubbery in the heat. I disbelieve my eyes, and strain to refocus them...but the precipice is real, and though it feels as though every molecule of moisture has been sucked out of me, the sight gives me another wind. I totter and lurch downwards, mentally munching nothingness. In most circumstances a bridge is a good trek spoiled, but here it is nirvana. I spy the span, and Walker standing waving back at me. I make it to the bridge, and give Walker a hug, and then find a spot to lay down in some shade. Anass stands above me, his mouth turned down at the corners like a cartoon. He grabs a palm-frond and waves it around my face, like an Orthodox priest blessing me with his thurible. Walker grabs my hand and fixes me with his eyes. "Dad, I was getting worried...and wanted to call for help, but cell phones don't work here." I can only grimace...my tongue is gluey with shame; my lips round to form my son's name, but no sound comes forth. My lips feel like dry corn husks chafing against each other. I feel as though the sun had ruthlessly charged through my body, and left something less than before. It burned my outer layer and left me floating numb, a derelict shell.

Walker fetches me the last of his water, and I drink it greedily. But my throat cries for more. Walker gently pries the water bottle from my rigid fingers. Anass tells me I was gone for four hours, and that he was about to head down to Akchour to find a landline and call for a rescue team.

I take a long rest, and Walker and Anass fetch more bottles of water, which I down as though they are miniatures. Then, with Walker helping me I slowly make my way down the path, like a battle-wounded soldier on retreat. When we get to the Akchour reservoir, both Walker and I pull off our clothes, and jump into the cold, cold waters. There is an overwhelming feeling of *Tissir*, an untranslatable Arabic word for a state of bliss and luck.

That evening, back in the powder-blue cocoon that is Chefchaouen, we all take dinner at an open-air restaurant in the Plaza Uta el-Hamman, across from toffee-colored walls of the 18th-century Kasbah. The legendary ruler Moulay Ismail built this Kasbah, but it is most noted for the hardheaded local chief, Abdu l-Karim, who was imprisoned within the walls in 1926 by Spanish troops. With his fall, the Spanish took over and held northern Morocco for the next 30 years. Now, it is a garden and a tourist attraction.

Between bites of our goat-meat tajine, washed down with freshly-squeezed orange juice (alcohol is prohibited here, though not apparently *kif*, which grows in abundance in fields surrounding the village), I ask Anass why he lied to me about so many things.

"You are strong, Mr. Richard. But as a guide, as a Moroccan, I was worried about you. I watched you the first hour, and saw someone more proud than wise. I did not think you would listen to my ideas. So, I tried to turn you around. These were my ways. I am sorry."

But I was glad to be alive, dining in a blue cloud, across from a Kasbah. Like the nomad, when there is no more, it is time to leave.

AFTERWORD

So, what is the modern Kasbah? It used to be a place for families, for safety, for travelers and traders to exchange goods, art, technologies, and disparate beliefs. It had clutches of rooms for many people, and they were all connected. It created a culture of people willing to accept unwelcome ideas, ones that sometimes shattered deeply held beliefs. Here is the nakedly revealed reality that in accommodating strangers we are brought to a crossroads of truth to power. It is at these crossroads that the foundations of the evolution of thought are laid—here are the encounters that take us to the permeable borders between stasis and understanding.

Wandering through the blades of dusty sunlight in the markets of Morocco, witnessing the mastery of craftsmen, delving into the deep history, and basking in the welcomes of new acquaintances, I was knocked over with a feeling of being part of something remarkable and deeply human. French travel writer André Chevrillon said about this land: "If such a world which shares so deeply the spirit of the past had disappeared two thousand years ago, we would have lost a certain understanding of the past and of ourselves, for we could never have recreated it. …But that it has survived until our own time, that we can see it, touch it, mix with its people, is a miracle that never ceases to astonish."

The paradox of the Kasbah was that it was both barbaric and domestic. It was a fortress, with one exit and entrance, designed to keep certain peoples outside its walls; yet it was also a place of gathering for nomads, and as such, a locus for the exchange of fresh ideas and different ways of thinking, as well as tapping into layers of accumulated wisdom. But in a way it makes sense. It is when a people feel safe and secure that they become open and receptive to different notions and mores; it is a vast and sheltering sky where bigotry, prejudice and demonization melt away. It is the sanctuary milieu that nurtures identity and tolerance, unnerves habits and perceptions, and leads to the evolution of thought and the breaking down of the walls within our minds.

It was many years ago that my friend Lew Greenwald tempted me with ideas of Morocco, and how it was a place that evoked something beyond thought and reason. Lew now pays rent everyday in the Kasbah in my heart.

In Morocco today the Kasbah is perhaps a synecdoche for the whole of the kingdom, a place secure in identity and thus unthreatened by those of different creed or kin. It is a world view developed through centuries of nomadic movement. It is a berth for people of all backgrounds and faiths to gather and share, a country that respects and celebrates the interconnectedness of the family of man. Morocco today, and always, is a Kasbah with an open door.

INDEX

INDEX

INDEX

INDEX

YOU'VE READ THE BOOK,
NOW GET THE DVD!

"Morocco: Quest for the Kasbah" is the latest episode in *Richard Bangs' Adventures with Purpose* American Public Television series. Produced by Small World Productions and co-produced by KCTS Seattle and Richard Bangs Productions, this one-hour documentary is now available for sale in either DVD or video format, with more than two hours of additional bonus footage for just $24.95 plus shipping.

Order through Small World Productions online at www.smarttravels.tv/adventure.htm, or call their toll-free number at 800/866-7425.

QUEST FOR THE KASBAH

QUEST FOR THE KASBAH

OPEN ROAD PUBLISHING

Open Road publishes travel guides to great destinations across the globe. Our books include:

• *Best Of* guides giving you the very best of countries, regions, states and cities worldwide—while at the same time telling you how to do it all in the time you have for your trip. We think most travel guides are just way too big, covering things you'll never get a chance to do. Our *Best Of* guides are the remedy, with beautiful color photos and maps throughout each book.

• *With Kids* guides for family travel, written by parents with an eye to what kids in particular will enjoy doing on their big adventure. Family-friendly hotels, restaurants, sights and activities are fully covered. Eye-popping color photos and maps in these books too!

• *Eating & Drinking* guides that are unique menu-readers to Paris, Italy and Spain. Can't figure out those strange words on the menu? These books are the solution, with thousands of menu items translated into English—plus restaurant suggestions, dining and pronunciation tips, and much more. Beautifully illustrated in color.

• *Travelogues*, of which the book you are now holding in your hands is the first in this exciting series of companion books to the PBS series *Richard Bangs' Adventures with Purpose*.

QUEST FOR THE KASBAH

ABOUT THE AUTHOR

Richard Bangs has often been called the father of modern adventure travel. He has spent more than 30 years as an explorer and communicator, and along the way he has led first descents of 35 rivers around the globe, including the Yangtze in China and the Zambezi in southern Africa.

Bangs has published more than one thousand magazine articles, 19 books, and a score of documentaries. He founded Sobek Expeditions, which later merged with Mountain Travel to become Mountain Travel Sobek—the leader in adventure travel. His

book *The Lost River: A Memoir of Life, Death and the Transformation of Wild Water* won the National Outdoor Book Award in the literature category. He is currently producing and hosting the PBS series *Richard Bangs' Adventures with Purpose*, of which this is the companion book to the Morocco special premiering in 2009.

photo by Laura Hubber

Future Morocco explorer Jasper Bangs

(photo by Laura Hubber)